D1120625

Endorsements

"*Oh, Happy Day!*...is a refreshing read in one sitting because you can't put this one down! Sallie Yusko, who's literally loved by thousands, is totally transparent with the subtle intention of teaching truth and dispensing wisdom for Christian living. The weaving of her humor keeps you laughing and learning. Truly a spoon full of sanguine sugar makes life's unavoidable medicine go down. I have known this mighty woman of God for twenty plus years, and she is delightfully powerful. Invite her to come speak. She's the real deal who talks just like she writes with wit and reality releasing healing and joy."

—**Jill Mitchell O'Brien** / President & Founder, Kingdom Connections International Inc., Houston, Texas

"Sallie Yusko's memoir, *Oh, Happy Day!* is a charming, sweet, and often heart-wrenching read. The author's transparency makes her so relatable and her story so valuable and usable by the Lord. I highly recommend it!"

—**Sylvia Bambola** / Award winning author of nine novels, including *Rebekah's Treasure* and *The Salt Covenants*

"Sallie Yusko is a positive and enthusiastic woman of God. *Oh, Happy Day!* chronicles her extraordinary journey of personal and pastoral leadership that gives the reader hope to succeed through the ups and downs of life. The author brilliantly weaves her own colorful life's experiences together with principles for living from the Word of God. Sallie is an encourager, and her book speaks plainly, with refreshing honesty, and a genuine interest in giving others hope and faith to succeed. Read this book and let Sallie lift your spirit and feed your soul."

—**Pastor Phil Derstine** / Christian Retreat Family Church, Bradenton, Florida, author of *7 Steps to Unconventional Soulwinning*

"This wonderful book conveys truth in both practical and spiritual ways. It is not religious 'fluff'; it is down-to-earth, yet simultaneously, it carries the reader up-to-heaven to see how these two worlds can blend in the life of a believer. You will benefit from reading it and you will probably want Sallie to come and speak in your church."

—**Mike Shreve** / Evangelist, author, and CEO of Deeper Revelation Books

"Sallie Yusko is an amazing woman of God! I should know. Over the last 20 years she has been a mentor, a spiritual mom, a confidant and friend. Through those years I have watched her grow in her knowledge and intimacy with the Father, as she has faced and overcome the many adversities that she willingly shares about in her book. Sallie is as transparent as she is encouraging as she pours herself into her writing. To read her story is to get to know her wit, charm, sense of humor, tenacity, grit, and faith for yourself; all the while finding yourself within the pages of this well written, woven testament of God's love and grace towards one of His own. On a more personal note, I know I would never have come into my own destiny without her faithful mentorship and sometimes stern but always loving corrections. She has been a true inspiration to me and my ministry and now it is my pleasure to share her with you! Read this book and be blessed, encouraged and inspired to reignite your love for the Father, the Son and the Holy Ghost!"

—**Dianna Leigh** / Founder of Global Esthers Ministries

"I love this book! It is compelling, fascinating, and humorous. I've been blessed to know Sallie for many years, but I did not know quite a few of the stories that she shared. To be honest, once I started reading the book, I could not put it down. Sallie relays to the reader of the miracles she and her family have experienced, and what steps led to those miracles. Her honesty is comforting and refreshing. *Oh, Happy Day!* would be a wonderful gift for a new bride, for someone who has experienced trauma or shame, or for a widow that is trying to cope with the loss of a spouse. She gives many tips on how to overcome in some very difficult situations. I recommend *Oh, Happy Day! Tell the Truth and Shame the Devil*, for all to read."

—**Susan Eaves** / Evangelist, motivational speaker, author, and life coach

Sallie Yusko

OH, HAPPY DAY!

Tell The Truth & Shame The Devil

Unless otherwise noted, all scriptures are from the NEW AMERICAN STANDARD BIBLE ®, Copyright© 1960, 1962, 1963, 1968, 1971, 1972, 1973, 1975, 1977, 1995 by The Lockman Foundation. Used by permission.

Scripture quotations marked (KJV) are taken from the KING JAMES VERSION, public domain.

Scripture quotations marked (NIV) are taken from THE HOLY BIBLE, NEW INTERNATIONAL VERSION®. Copyright© 1973, 1978, 1984, 2011 by Biblica, Inc.™ Used by permission of Zondervan.

Author contact info (Sallie Yusko)

Email: salliemary@gmail.com

Individuals and church groups may order books from Sallie Yusko directly, or from the publisher. Retailers and wholesalers should order from our distributors. Refer to the Deeper Revelation Books website for distribution information, as well as an online catalog of all our books.

Published by:

Deeper Revelation Books

Revealing "the deep things of God" (1 Cor. 2:10)

P.O. Box 4260

Cleveland, TN 37320

Phone: 423-478-2843

Website:www.deeperrevelationbooks.org

Email: info@deeperrevelationbooks.org

Deeper Revelation Books assists Christian authors in publishing and distributing their books. Final responsibility for design, content, permissions, editorial accuracy, and doctrinal views, either expressed or implied, belongs to the author.

Table of Contents

Dedication

To my late husband,
Al Yusko, of over fifty-three years,
who has always encouraged
and believed in me.
You have been my biggest fan
and cheerleader.
Looking forward to that day
when we will once again be reunited
for all eternity.
I will love you forever.

Foreword

When I first met Sallie, she was a pastor's wife in our hometown of Bradenton, Florida. Her husband, Al, taught in our Institute of Ministry at Christian Retreat and they were active leaders in our church community. But I didn't really get to know Sallie until she became a member of my women's lunch group, a diverse collection of busy women who met to fellowship, eat, swap stories about our lives, and of course, pray.

Cute and blonde with a bubbly personality and easy laugh, Sallie lit up the room when she walked in the door. I soon learned she and I shared a common interest (besides discovering new and fun places to eat), and that was writing. Sallie showed up at my Writer's Workshop at Christian Retreat more than once and soaked in the information. Despite her expressed feelings of inadequacy, she felt led of God to write her life story and I encouraged her to begin. And she did.

After reading *Oh, Happy Day!* I realized how much Sallie's life deserved a book. Beneath that delicate exterior was one tough, resilient girl! There was so much I didn't know about the challenges she overcame, from growing up with an alcoholic mother who had been married multiple times, to navigating the ups and downs of ministry life. Wow! I couldn't stop reading.

In *Oh, Happy Day!* Sallie "tells the truth" with candor and humor. She doesn't mince words, and tells it like it is, in her own engaging style. Sprinkled through with Scripture and lessons learned, it's a great read, offering hope and inspiration to anyone dealing with fear, guilt and real-life challenges. As you read Sallie's story, enjoy the journey and expect miracles in your own life!

—**Joanne Derstine Curphey** / Author and Director of Communications, Christian Retreat, Bradenton, Florida

Chapter 1

The Italian Who Wouldn't Take "No" for an Answer

The night was dark and foreboding…there were no lights anywhere and the stars seemed to be hiding. There we were in the middle of the Mohave Desert in the month of August, where it felt almost as hot as hell itself. The mood was ominous and eerie. We had just left Los Angeles, California, a few hours earlier, and we were off to Vegas.

I was scared!

I know I don't have that "extreme" gene they talk about; sometimes, I think I had the "chicken" gene.

We pulled up to what looked like an abandoned, old shack, when just then, a wrinkly, old man came out the door shouting, "Why are you on my property, and what do ya want?" It reminded me of an old TV series, *The Twilight Zone*.

Albert, my soon-to-be husband, explained to the old man that we really weren't paying much attention to the gas gauge, and we were paying more attention to each other. Frankly, I don't think he was the least bit amused.

Albert said, "We were on our way to Las Vegas to get married, when suddenly, our car just ran out of gas." Apparently, the old man at this time felt some type of sympathy, or he just seemed to know we needed a lot of help (which, of course, we did). So, a bit reluctantly, he let us use his telephone. (That was the pre-cell phone era.)

We called Triple-A (AAA), only to find out that the card in Al's wallet had expired a few days earlier. Oh, great! What now?

The old man upon hearing this said that he could give us some extra gas that he had stored in his garage, enough to get us to the Las Vegas Strip, which was about a half-hour away. He wanted $25, which seemed like a thousand dollars at the time. We paid him the money and off we went, happy to have gas once again.

Just as we were approaching the Las Vegas Strip, that same, familiar sound of "spit, spat, spurt" became clear. Oh no! The old man did not give us enough gas. We barely had enough to glide into the first service station on fumes. Nevertheless, we were finally at the beginning of the famous Las Vegas Strip, and despite everything that had already taken place in the course of that day, we were very happy to have finally arrived at our destination.

Just a few hours earlier, I must have looked a sight, at least by gauging the looks I was getting from bystanders and the receptionist at the opposite end of the counter. My mouth was wide open…I was staring in shock and disbelief at what I had just heard; the man I was about to marry told the clerk at the City Hall that his name was Albert! Suspiciously, I pointed out, "I thought your name was Alan."

"That's okay; I like Alan," he responded.

"Well," I said, "I have been calling you by the name of Alan for months on the phone before we went out!" That didn't seem to faze him in the least. Next, I asked him if he was going to call his mother, and he said, "No, at least not

"What do you mean your name is not Alan? And what do you mean you are not going to tell your mother?"

right now." I thought that was strange...until I met his mother later on. She happened to find out from his roommate that he had gone off to get married when she tried to call him at his apartment. Well, you can imagine what must have been going through her head. As a mother myself, I can understand the feelings she must have had.

My mother and stepfather knew that we were going to go and get married. They gave us some money to elope. My stepfather was ecstatic because he was very cheap. He told my mother that I could wear my tennis shoes with my prom dress (maybe now it's fashionable, but it was not then). He did not want to pay for shoes, thinking enough was already spent on the dress. He was so happy that he got away with not having to pay for a big wedding, even though my mother would have paid for it. He married her because she had money. A big wedding never would have worked anyway, because there were just too many stepfathers and stepmothers in the equation due to multiple marriages of my mother and birth father. The mailman used to get confused, because there were so many different last names on the mailbox.

"No! I don't want to go out with you; you are not my type. Stop calling me!" These were the words that I was sure would turn off even the most ardent suitor. However, I had grossly misjudged the Italian who would not take "no" for an answer.

I can't tell you how many times I repeated those same words. Finally, I stopped answering the phone. When "Alan" would call, I pleaded with my mother to tell him that I was not home.

You would think that would be the end of it.

Case closed, right? Not so.

During these frequent phone calls, a beautiful relationship (unknown to me) was being formed between "Alan" and my mother. Mother was always known for her soft and tender heart.

She finally firmly said to me that when the next call came, and it did, "I will not lie for you anymore, Sallie, get on the phone and talk to this nice, young man. You are being extremely rude!" Begrudgingly, I took the phone. The power of persistence, and the Italian who wouldn't take "no" for an answer, finally won in the end.

Truth be told, I was just plain worn out. I could not believe anyone would spend that much time pursuing someone who constantly and emphatically said "No!"

Al's continual persistence was amazing to me in that he just never gave up. It sparked quite an interest within me as to what this

> **The power of persistence, and the Italian who wouldn't take "no" for an answer, finally won in the end.**

type of person was anyway; certainly, one that did not give up. That much I knew!

I am reminded of the unrighteous judge and the widow in the Bible who continually kept coming to him seeking legal protection. Even though he did not fear God, or respect man, he was unwilling to give it to her.

> *"Yet because this widow bothers me, I will give her legal protection, otherwise by continually coming she will wear me out."* (Luke 18:5)

Yes, I was for sure being slowly worn out by his continual persistence over many months. At long last, I conceded to have a date with this very persuasive, young man from Connecticut.

When I first saw him, it was in a Hollywood nightclub on the Sunset Strip, where a lot of the girls from Glendale used to go and meet up with friends and socialize. Our hometown had an ordinance against dancing. So, my friends and I would go to Hollywood to dance the "surfers' stomp." Oh Lord, am I ever dating myself! Well, I didn't see myself as a very good dancer, and I really had no interest in going. But this particular

Saturday night, my girlfriend begged me to come. She said, "Don't worry about getting in, because my boyfriend is the bouncer and he will let us in." None of us were twenty-one years of age. I said, "Alright, I will go."

That evening, the nightclub was exceptionally crowded. I was grateful, because I felt my dancing abilities, or lack of abilities, would less likely be noticed on the dance floor with so many others dancing. When the singer, Trini Lopez, who was famous for the song "Lemon Tree," took a break, I found myself sitting in a booth across from Al. It was not until seven years later, that the Lord brought to my recollection what happened at that moment. This thought came to my mind clearly out of the blue, "The man sitting directly across from you is going to be your husband." Although the thought was as clear as a bell, I dismissed it. Later that evening, I found out that my girlfriend gave Al my phone number. After several months of him calling me, we finally went out on a date. I am reminded of what my minister friend, Kevin Zadai, always says: "It's all rigged!"

SIX WEEKS LATER...

We were standing at the Justice of the Peace in Las Vegas, Nevada, saying our marriage vows. The witnesses consisted of the secretary and one other employee who remained present during the ceremony.

Celebrating my birthday for the first time with my husband

They were quick to offer their "advice" as soon as the "I do's" were said. Their counsel was simply, "If it doesn't work out, you can get a 'quickie divorce' in just a few weeks in Reno."

We really must have looked pitiful, and oh, we were so very young. These so-called "negative words of advice" were the "first words" we heard as husband and wife, and we were about to embark upon the very beginning of this marital journey.

I think I was numb, probably comatose.

Each one of us brought more baggage into the marriage than would hold Imelda Marcos' shoes. For the reader who is too young to remember, she was the wife of a former dictator of the Philippines (1965-1986). When she was questioned about her extravagant lifestyle, and her three thousand pairs of shoes, she was quick to respond, "I do not have 3,000 pairs of shoes, I have 1,060."

Our ride to Vegas was worse than I previously mentioned: we had two flat tires, along with a fan belt that kept slipping and coming off my red Chevy Corvair. By the time we arrived, we had run out of gas, not just once, but twice!

It had only been a few, short hours since we left Los Angeles when "Alan" (later known as Albert) and I set out on our trek to Las Vegas to get married. Hesitantly, I had switched from calling him Alan to Albert. I really did like the name Alan better, however. It was so funny to me, that name, "Albert."

During the entire car ride from Los Angeles, California, I was pondering how this was all going to turn out, and at the same time, wondering what my life was going to be like from that time forth. One thing I knew for sure…it would never be the same again.

That was the beginning of what was to be a very wild ride for the next five decades.

What a journey I had embarked upon! That was the beginning of what was to be a very wild ride for the next five decades.

I was young, pregnant, and scared…while at the same time, feeling an underlying sense of shame and embarrassment.

All the hopes and dreams I had in a childhood vision of a perfect, little family, like the families I had seen on TV growing up, were suddenly and completely shattered. A myriad of emotions were rapidly swirling around me, all clamoring for my attention. One moment I felt happy, the next moment, I felt helpless and hopeless, all the while being unable to see beyond my present circumstances.

How could this be? My "perfect" little plan of marriage and life as an adult was not starting out the way I had hoped; it all seemed to be falling apart.

For the next several years, I lived under a cloud of shame. Eventually, I began to feel safe enough to start letting the numbness of this self-imposed, emotional Novocain wear off. I ever so gingerly let the Holy Spirit come into those areas of my heart that were off limits for so long. I have heard it said that, "The teacher shows up when the student is ready."

Well, I was ready!

> *Instead of your shame you will have a*
> *double portion, and instead of humiliation*
> *they will shout for joy over their portion*
> *Therefore, they will possess a double portion*
> *in their land.*   (Isaiah 61:7)

The Holy Spirit began to reveal more and more of God's amazing love for me. He began showing me how walking in truth and light will always bring victory and healing, when we earnestly seek and desire change.

Sometimes, we cover up, deny, ignore, or just hope that difficult and painful situations will go away because it's in the past, right? Deep down, we need to let the Holy Spirit search our hearts so that He can bring closure and healing to those wounded areas of our souls.

In my generation, being pregnant out of wedlock was very shameful. Many girls in my high school would suddenly disappear as it were out of thin air and then suddenly reappear months later. That was before abortion was legalized. I don't know where they all went. I think some went to homes for pregnant girls, and I'm sure some had illegal abortions, but it was all "hush, hush" and very secretive. It's almost laughable to some today. Sad to say, this has become the norm in our culture.

The devil held this over my head for decades.

When past issues are brought to the light and dealt with, then the magnificent, transforming love and power of God Himself will bring such overflowing joy to your heart that you will begin to experience rivers of living water flowing through every fiber of your being. The enemy, Satan, the god of this world, can never use any of **God ALWAYS has a great plan for your life!** those "dealt-with-issues" in your life to harass you ever again!

God ALWAYS has a great plan for your life!

Seek Him with all your heart!

> *"For I know the plans that I have for you,*
> *declares the Lord, plans for welfare and not*
> *for calamity to give you a future and a hope."*
>
> (Jeremiah 29:11)

Dinner show in Las Vegas featuring the singer,
Jack Jones, on our wedding night

Chapter 2

The Days of Wine and Roses

*T*he *Days of Wine and Roses* was a film that came out in 1962. It was a very popular movie in that day, and had several nominations, including one for best actor and best actress. The original music was by Henry Mancini. The storyline was about a husband and wife, and how their marriage and lives had completely deteriorated because of alcoholism.

Because I identified with so many things that were portrayed in this movie, it was painful for me to watch.

> *"Pain has an element of blank; it cannot recollect when it began, or if there were a day when it was not."* — Emily Dickinson[1]

As I look back over my life, I realize I spent most of it in what I call a 'Novocain state.' I was numb most of the time. I realize that this was probably a pretty good protection and shield from most of the heartache and pain I would have to walk through as a child.

My parents were certainly not the "conventional" type, especially in the 50s. Television mothers of the 1950s through the early 70s were "perfect," or so I thought. They wore high heels and dresses, not a hair out of place. They were perfectly dressed, perfectly coiffed, and always perfectly pleasant. They would carry freshly baked cookies to the door, while greeting their smiling, charming children coming home from school.

However, this scenario did not exactly play out in my life.

I thought almost every family in America lived like this and I could not understand why God had forsaken me. "Why God, why? Why do I have to have such a messed-up family?"

"Do you hear me at all God?" I wondered, "Are you up there, God?"

You see, my mother would just get in the car and drive. Drunk or sober, she drove! Thankfully, no one was ever injured or killed, and this was before there were any strict drunk driving laws.

"I don't know how to drive!" I would be screaming this as I woke up from a reoccurring nightmare as a child. I remember waking up in a literal sweat-filled panic.

I would dream that my mother and I were in the car and she would be driving while extremely drunk and ready to pass out, and then I would wake up. I knew I couldn't drive; my little, curly head could barely reach the steering wheel. The responsibility and fear I was feeling were beyond overwhelming.

I remember being a very terrified eight-year-old girl, fearful that my mom might pass out while she drove, knowing full well that I didn't know how to drive a car. This was a frightening, sometimes recurring dream that I experienced as a young child.

A few years passed, and indeed, it was a rare day when you would find my mother sober.

I felt like I could not tell a soul, so I tried to "cover it up" because it was so shameful to me. I really thought that no one in the whole, wide world would even marry me if they knew these things about my family. Lies, lies, lies, of the enemy!

> **Telling the truth and shaming the devil is what I do now.**

Telling the truth and shaming the devil is what I do now; I shame him! What he meant for evil, God used for good! The devil is the one who wants to keep you defeated, discouraged, and sitting in the dark.

> *And they overcame him because of the blood
> of the Lamb and because of the word of their
> testimony.* (Revelation 12:11)

"Why God," I would ask, "Why? Why does everyone seem to have such normal families, where their mother hasn't been married five times and their father, seven times?" Don't forget, that was in the 50s culture, and that was not the norm.

One day, one of my mother's friends from AA (Alcoholics Anonymous) greeted me, only to tell me that my mother had been picked up for a drunk driving charge. She then told me that I would be spending the night with her, because my mother was being held at the county jail. I really didn't know this lady very well, but one thing I knew for sure was that I didn't like her.

My mother and stepfather

It seems as if my mother only found the ones at AA who still wanted to drink, and therefore, found more drinking buddies rather than friends that wanted to stay sober. I felt this woman was one of the former, rather than the latter.

Alcoholics are very clever people. My mother had all kinds of hiding places for her booze. But this one day, she wasn't so clever, as you will soon see. When I came home from school, I never knew if I would find my mother drunk and passed out on the floor or if she would even be home. Rarely did I invite anyone over, because I never knew what I would find, or what to expect. When I did invite someone over, I pleaded with my mother to stay sober, and hoped and prayed for the best.

One day, I planned on bringing my best friend home from school to spend the night. This was very brave I thought, because I knew I was leaving myself in a vulnerable state. Finally, someone could spend the night when I wasn't wetting the bed. I was so happy about that, to be sure.

What I saw next were my worst fears coming true: liquor bottles. I just wanted to die; the embarrassment was over-whelming for this pre-teen girl. There they all were lined up in a neat little row behind the drapes of a very large, eight-foot sliding glass window right in front where all passersby could see. I secretly prayed that my best friend would not "see" all those bottles, but in my heart, I knew that she did see them. She was just too kind, and too good of a friend to say anything. I knew deep down that she felt my embarrassment and pain.

My mother often admitted to me that she could not make good choices when it came to choosing friends, or husbands for that matter. She would often tell me how lucky I was to have such a nice husband, and not to worry about my mother-in-law. She said, "I have had lousy husbands, but great mothers-in-law, and Sallie, it's far better to have a great husband!"

She was married five times and married one husband twice. My dad actually surpassed my mother in the marriage department, for he was divorced and remarried seven times.

Margaret Anderson's children on *Father Knows Best*, a television show in the fifties and sixties, never saw drunken parents and divorce was never even mentioned.

The television mothers of that era never had anything dirty touch their carpets, children, or clothes. I really thought everyone's family life was just like the one I watched on TV: wonderful and perfect.

It was only as an adult that I came to realize that the father on *Father Knows Best*, in real life, was an alcoholic. I was shocked and saddened hearing the news. It was just so hard to believe, especially after spending a great deal of my childhood watching a show that I thought portrayed real life, albeit not mine.

One day, I recall waiting the entire day until nightfall, sitting at the curb of an ice-skating rink in Denver, Colorado, waiting for my mother to pick me up.

Finally, when it grew dark, she showed up, drunk, of course!

I was determined at a very young age, that when I became an adult, my life would never, ever, take the same route as my parents or stepparents. Whatever it would take, I was determined to make my marriage work, and to bring stability to my children. I promised myself that I would never willingly let my children experience the same things I did in my childhood. I was going to cook for them. I was going to make them lunches with their names written on their lunch bags to take to school; just the way my childhood friends' mothers did. I was going to pick them up, and always be on time. Never would I leave them waiting or wondering where I was. Yes, that was the plan!

> **I promised myself that I would never willingly let my children experience the same things I did in my childhood.**

My last two years in high school were spent in public school. It was during that time that mother's binges and the ensuing chaos started to surface more frequently. My daily diet on most days consisted of eating chocolate frosting right out of the can, and English muffins loaded with butter. Of course, I can't deny that I liked chocolate frosting and English muffins, because I did. Actually, truth be known, I did pretty much what I felt like, because there were no boundaries per se and very little, if any, restrictions. Mother cooked occasionally, and it was quite good when she did. She mastered the art of "doctoring up" already prepared foods and making them delicious in some of her better moments.

ONLY GOD CAN CHANGE PEOPLE

You really can't change anyone. I tried so hard to help my mom, at a very early age. I was "the mother," she was "the child." This was an extremely dysfunctional role reversal at its worst, creating a very heavy burden for any child of any age.

That's why I love the phrase, "It's never too late to have a happy childhood."

It wasn't until I had been married for many decades, yes, that's right, decades, that I could go into a public restroom without first telling my husband to wait right there at the door for me until I came out. Coming out and not finding him would foster the feelings of the "fear of abandonment" all over again. I know this might seem like overreacting for those who have never experienced this, but to those who have, you know the exact truth of what I am saying, and probably realize this is almost an understatement.

For my father and my mother have forsaken
me, but the Lord will take me up.
(Psalms 27:10)

When I returned from my week-long honeymoon in Las Vegas, my girlfriends gave me a wedding shower, and my dear mother, once again, showed up late and very drunk. Every time something important was going to take place: holidays, birthdays, you name it, you could count on the fact that she would not be sober. I secretly hoped that this day, which was so important to me, would be different.

I always felt like I had to be overly responsible since most of the people in my life were overly NOT responsible! I can see how this led not only to unrealistic expectations, but to control issues in me. The Lord, in His grace and mercy, revealed this to me later in my life. In fact, it was about ten years after I had become a Christian. One of the conference speakers at our church suggested that I buy this certain book on co-dependency. I just happened to mention very briefly in passing that my parents drank.

"Well, that was really it!" I thought to myself. "This is just great; the first time I 'test the waters' so to speak and mention anything about my past, this lady thinks I have a problem. Good grief!" I was mad at myself for letting my guard down and becoming so vulnerable.

I never talked about my childhood because of the shame and embarrassment.

I bought the book, and much to my surprise and great dismay, I realized almost everything that was written described my life. "God," I screamed, "That's not fair! I'm the responsible one; I don't drink!"

God was speaking through this author. He gently and lovingly continued the healing process of those areas in my life that were severely wounded.

When the Spirit of God is prompting you to do something that you would rather not do in your flesh: never, ever, hold back! Countless lives could be forever changed. I'm so grateful to that lady who spoke at the church conference for sharing information that she knew I needed. She didn't seem to worry about whether or not I might be offended or think less of her. Thank God for people who love you and love God, enough to be obedient and speak truth into your life.

Faithful are the wounds of a friend, but deceitful are the kisses of an enemy.
(Proverbs 27:6)

Parts of that book made me really mad! But then, I got glad!

What I discovered through reading this book is that the non-drinker, who is living with an alcoholic, has just as many problems or issues as the alcoholic, due to all of the dysfunction, drama, and chaos that is experienced. Well, that was a hard pill to swallow initially; especially when you consider yourself to be the sober, sane, rational one! You know, if God showed us everything that was wrong with us all at once, we would probably faint, and not be able to bear it.

The truth will always set you free, even if it hurts at first.

God takes the broken places and pieces of your life and brings redemption and restoration. He knows and feels your pain.

For we do not have a high priest who cannot sympathize with our weaknesses, but One who has been tempted in all things as we are, yet without sin. (Hebrews 4:15)

I was a very serious child and did not laugh much. I can remember someone saying to me in the hall of my public high school, "You never smile."

That statement was so surprising to me, because I really did try to hide the sadness that I was feeling at home. However, our feelings have a tendency to betray us, and show up on our countenance without asking our permission.

Imagine that!

People today tell me that I am "funny," and that I make them laugh. Now, I am laughing and smiling most of the time. God has given me unbelievable joy, for in His Presence there is fullness of joy!

He is no respecter of persons. What He has done for me, He will surely do for you! Jesus makes all things brand new, because of His great love and mercy for all mankind.

*"And I will restore to you the years that the
locust hath eaten, the cankerworm, and the
caterpillar, and the palmerworm."*
(Joel 2:25 KJV)

How many years of your past life were eaten up by the
cankerworms of sin, rebellion, and dysfunction?

God will restore your wasted years. He has restored my
soul and given me a "childlike" spirit, causing the old things to
pass away.

*He leads me beside quiet waters. He restores
my soul.* (Psalms 23:2-3)

*Therefore if anyone is in Christ, he is a new
creature; the old things passed away; behold,
new things have come.* (2 Corinthians 5:17)

Chapter 3

The Nanny

*J*ennie was the sweetest lady that God ever put on this earth. I called her "Nanny," for that's who she was in our family. She was my nanny and my angel.

I remember crying at the table one evening after our dinner was served. My father knew why I was crying, and he had already tried to explain to me on other occasions what he was about to tell me once again. "Why did she have to eat in the kitchen by herself after making us a beautiful dinner?" I wondered. "The 'help,' Sallie, are never to eat with the rest of the family at the dining room table for dinner." My seven-year-old mind could not understand such foolishness. After all, Jennie was like my mother, and she was a very important part of my life. I felt that was a perfectly stupid rule, and I didn't like it one bit. Jennie was my very best friend.

My nanny and brother, with his little playmate

My first experience with the love of God came through this simple, uneducated woman that God placed in our home. She was born and raised on a farm in Iowa, and never married or had children of her own.

My childhood perception was that sometimes my family looked at her differently, but I thought she was the most wonderful person in the whole wide world.

"God sees not as man sees, for man looks at the outward appearance, but the Lord looks at the heart." (1 Samuel 16:7)

Jennie faithfully went to church on Sundays, which was her only day off from working and living in our home. She always talked about Jesus, and how she wanted to marry Billy Graham. She would come home at day's end with a "Cup of Gold" candy bar for me. I was so delighted, and oh, how I looked forward to that delicious treat every week. I know we must have seemed beyond all hope. Her great faith and perseverance enabled her to sow "seeds of life" into our family. She never stopped praying for us.

We became her family and she literally gave her life for us. She loved us so unconditionally; it was absolutely amazing to me. I can remember, at times, being an absolute brat. I would order her around, telling her to "get me this" or "make me that." One time, and one time only, I told her to "shut up"!

Well, I am here to tell you that I learned my lesson on respect real quick and real well when my German father arrived home from work at the end of that day, and found out what I had done. My mother could not deal with most things that she considered difficult in this life, so she would always say, "Wait until your father comes home, and he can deal with it."

I remember running up the stairs as fast as my little legs would go, because I knew I was going to get spanked (something that is almost a foreign concept in present-day society). My father chased me up the winding staircase in our home with a hairbrush and spanked my little behind. Looking back as an adult, I have a tremendous amount of respect for all authority, and especially God as a result of that one incident. I considered that to be an invaluable life lesson, and I am very grateful for it, although at the time, I'm sure that was not my sentiment.

For those whom the Lord loves he disciplines. (Hebrews 12:6)

All discipline for the moment seems not to be joyful, but sorrowful; yet to those who have been trained by it, afterwards it yields the peaceful fruit of righteousness. (Hebrews 12:11)

Jennie's love and kindness for me never wavered; it was always unconditional, no matter how I acted. I look back and realize that she really was just like Jesus, filled with His Spirit, flowing in His love.

It was twenty years later before I came to know Jesus Christ as my personal Lord and Savior. Her sacrificial life and tireless efforts spent in prayer for my family were not in vain. She no longer worked for us, except to clean sometimes, along with some other cleaning jobs she managed to get. I knew she didn't have much money, and it seemed like my family was not going to take care of her; they were always moving, and marrying, and could barely take care of themselves.

In later years, around the time I got married, Jennie had become an old woman, living in an apartment in Glendale, California. I remember always worrying about who was going to take care of her in her old age. These were recurring thoughts that periodically surfaced. It made me sad.

In that same year, Southern California experienced another large earthquake, over 7.0 on the Richter scale. Jennie lived on the second floor of an apartment building, and half of her living quarters were demolished by the earthquake, leaving her stranded two stories high.

Who would have thought this earthquake would turn into a blessing for her. God is so good! As a result of this, she was

Not one sparrow falls to the ground without His notice.

transferred to the most luxurious assisted living facility in the state of California. It looked like a very upscale hotel, with impeccable furnishings, thick and lush carpeting, beautiful oil paintings on every wall, and brilliantly lit chandeliers lighting up the foyer.

Not one sparrow falls to the ground without His notice.

> *"Are not two sparrows sold for a cent? And yet not one of them will fall to the ground apart from your Father. But the very hairs of your head are all numbered. So do not fear; you are more valuable than many sparrows."*
> (Matthew 10:29-31)

While living in Rockland County, New York, I wrote Jennie, my nanny, a long letter and told her just how much I loved her, and how I appreciated all she had done for our family. I was able, for the first time, to tell her that God had indeed answered her prayers. I, too, had come to know her Jesus.

She was growing senile at the time, but I believe that God spoke to her spirit, letting her know that her sacrificial life was not in vain. I also believe that this simple woman's love, prayers, and obedience will be forever memorialized throughout all eternity, as a sweet-smelling fragrance. God did not forget Jennie! Oh, how I loved her!

> *For God is not unjust so as to forget your work and the love which you have shown toward His name, in having ministered and in still ministering to the saints.* (Hebrews 6:10)

Chapter 4

I Will Be Happy When...

Mother's mantra: "If we just move somewhere else or if I marry someone else, I know things will get better, and I will be happy."

My grandmother died from the 1918 flu epidemic, leaving my grandfather to raise two little girls. My grandfather was in his sixties at the time; a great deal older than my grandmother who was only in her thirties. A lady named Pearl Wallace, who had no children of her own, came with her husband to live in my grandfather's home, helping to raise the children; my mother was just nine months old and her sister was three.

Pearl disliked my father immensely and was always telling my mother to divorce him. Apparently, the final straw came when he hit my mother over the head with a liquor bottle; Pearl's story, of course. There were other scenarios that I later found out about from my brother.

What I had known about family life up to this point abruptly changed. My mother divorced my father, her third husband, when I was seven-years-old, and my life was quickly filling up with insecurities.

I had to leave a very beautiful home on a picturesque street in Glendale, California, one that could have easily resembled something right out of a Norman Rockwell painting. I loved all the flowers in our three-tiered backyard: camellias, roses, and other flowering bushes. My nanny, Jennie, would give me a glass jar, one in which she had poked holes in the lid. She knew I loved to catch bees in the backyard. Through the glass jar, I could look and study the bees for hours. Then, I would open the lid and release them until another day. They fascinated me, and miraculously, I never got a bee sting!

My mother, brother, and me, in happier times

There were some good memories, and I actually did some "kid" stuff: playing games like 'kick the can" and "hide and seek." I no longer felt overly responsible for everyone and everything.

But that all changed quickly...

Mother, divorced again, moved us to an apartment in South Pasadena, where there were few children and no one my age to play with. My brother would sometimes play with me, but with a strict, disciplined father out of our home, it became at times a "free for all," because my dear mother was incapable of bringing discipline into our lives. I know we were quite a handful, to say the least.

One day, my brother and I were outside playing, and he wanted to try out his bow and arrow set. Who was the best person to try it out on? Me! "Don't worry, I won't hit you with this arrow, just stand there and be still," he would say. Almost immediately, the tip of the arrow was penetrating the top of my right foot next to my toes.

Soon after that, my brother was sent away to military school. I was then alone with my mother and this horrible dog she named Rags. I love all animals, especially dogs, but this particular dog brings back bad memories. He was an exceptionally large standard black poodle that remained untrained the entire time he lived with us. He was always jumping on everything and I'm sure he thought our entire apartment was his bathroom. Enough said. I will leave the rest to your imagination.

Uprooted once again almost one year later, we left South Pasadena, California, as mother decided things would be better in Colorado. Rags did not go. Mother knew that it would never work. Thank God for revelation! I have no idea who took the dog, and I am sure I did not care!

Denver, here we come! What a group! My mother never liked to be alone, so she invited her man-hating, divorced girlfriend, and two of her children to travel with us. The entire time, this lady talked about how horrible men were, because her husband had left her and their six children for a younger woman.

We all set off for this wild adventure in one car: with the children fighting, poking, jabbing, screaming almost the entire trip to Denver. The two mothers appeared oblivious, periodically blurting out, "Shut up, or else!"

ALWAYS LEAVING ON "MOTHER'S WHIMS"

Oh, how I hated moving! This meant once again being uprooted and going to another new school, which often left me feeling helpless and stupid. My mother's philosophy was always the same: "If I just move somewhere else or marry someone else... everything will get better."

I never did seem to get caught up in my studies, and I was always the "new kid on the block." But eventually, I learned to adapt. I knew that soon, I would be grown up, and I purposed in my heart that when that time came, things would be different. I would never willingly subject my children to the pain I experienced.

We only stayed in Denver for one year, and then once again, came back to Southern California, where my mother got married again. That marriage did not last long, but she ended up marrying my stepfather a second time, a few years later.

Mother decided that life would get better if she took a very long cruise to South America after divorcing my stepfather. She was going to take my brother and me out of school a few months early before summer vacation, and one thing I knew for sure is that I was not about to go! Fifth grade was the only grade I remember liking. I was the "teacher's pet," and I was actually learning something and starting to feel somewhat confident.

My dad lived about forty-five minutes away from my school in La Canada, California. He lived in North Hollywood with my stepmother. They let me come and stay with them and agreed to drive me to and from school each day while my mother and brother were cruising in South America. That was great news for me!

Knowing that my dad was a strict disciplinarian meant that I would not have the same freedom I had living with my mother. I knew I was not going to like that part of the arrange-

My dad and me in 1970

ment. However, I was obedient and respectful to my dad, as I always remembered that he said what he meant and meant what he said. I did not dare disobey or act bratty in front of him.

My time spent in North Hollywood

ended up much better than expected. I learned more in the remainder of that year than possibly any other school year, until I got to college. My dad also painstakingly set the clock three times during the course of a night to come and wake me up and take me to the bathroom. I was such a heavy sleeper (I slept through 7.5 earthquakes); I just could not wake up to go to the bathroom. I would often dream that I was already in the bathroom, and I thought I was until I felt the wet sheets in the morning. It was awful! By the time my mother and brother came back, I no longer wet the bed, and I am thankful to my dad for helping me overcome that burden in my young life.

My brother is five years my senior and was mostly away in boarding schools or the army when the drinking grew more intense. My uncle and mother enlisted him in the army at age eighteen. I am grateful that my brother never fully experienced the literal "Days of Wine and Roses." Thankfully, he missed the majority of the devastation that alcoholism brings into a family.

Scottsdale, Arizona, here I come. Yippee! Boarding school! I was ecstatic!

My trunk was packed with Levi's jeans, snap button-down shirts, cowboy boots, and tennis clothes. I was more than ready to go!

Oh, did I have fun! It sure was a lot better than finding my mother's hidden liquor bottles and pouring the alcohol down the drain, which had become an almost daily ritual.

I got shipped off to a boarding school in Scottsdale, Arizona, for the seventh grade. I came to find out, my best girlfriend and roommate had eleven stepmothers. Wow, how about that! I was starting to feel more and more at home. My other friend's mother married and divorced her husband eight times. Yes, you read it right, the same husband, eight times. It made the national news! My husband said, "Isn't that your good friend's mother from boarding school that you told me about?" I said, "Yes, that is her alright."

I was beginning to feel a weird "normal" in this new environment of breathtaking sunsets and beautiful cacti. I did not really enjoy those pesky, little scorpions that seemed to be everywhere. Yes, I was starting to feel more comfortable, and less isolated.

Today, that might not seem like such a big deal, but for me and my generation, it was huge. There just were

I did not really enjoy those pesky, little scorpions that seemed to be everywhere.

not that many people around that had multiple mothers and fathers, unless they were movie stars.

It was only when I started attending boarding school with the rich and the famous, that my perception about reality gradually started to change.

I didn't learn too much (practically nothing academically) at this co-educational boarding school in Scottsdale, but the parties were great and oh, did I have fun! I learned to play tennis, go shopping at Goldwater's department store, blow smoke rings, ride horses, and do water ballet, among a host of other fun things.

I would spend my afternoons in the "Concho Room." This was a room for the teens at the school with a soda fountain, juke box, and padded leather booths in which to sit with your friends. We would drink cokes and shakes and listen to the popular music of the 50s. No wonder the adjustment to an all-girls, Catholic boarding school the following year was like a prison camp to me. A severe adjustment would be a definite understatement!

Most of my growing-up years were spent changing schools almost every year, with two years at a clip being the longest amount of time spent in any school.

THE DREADED PHONE CALL

Shortly before Thanksgiving in 1970, I received that dreaded middle-of-the-night phone call from my stepfather, telling me that my fifty-two-year-old mother was dead.

Several weeks before she died, my mother called me on the telephone and said that my stepfather had pulled the garage door down hard over her head while she was standing there. She said, "I had to literally jump out of the way because I felt it was done on purpose. It seemed like he was trying to kill me." I don't know if she willingly took her own life that fateful day in November, or if my stepfather slipped into her drink the medication that he knew would kill her if it was mixed with alcohol.

It's a curious thing, because I always felt that my stepfather was at least on my side, especially knowing the devastating effects alcoholism had on our lives. It was during that period of time that my mother was trying very hard to stop drinking, but my stepfather did not like the control he was losing over her life.

Why? Because for the first time in her life, she decided to stand up to him and would not allow herself to be abused and controlled. He did not like that! One evening, when she was standing her ground, I happened to be visiting. What I witnessed was shocking and almost hard to believe at first. Without any warning, he went into a complete rage, spitting out profanities and hurling the contents of his drink right into her face saying, "I know you want a drink. Go and get one."

It was at that moment, I finally realized that he never wanted her sober after all.

Later, the autopsy showed that she died from alcohol and barbiturate poisoning. I never got closure. My stepfather had my mother quickly cremated, and I never did get to see her. He had her body removed from the house almost immediately. When my husband and I arrived, my mother had already been removed from the premises, and my stepfather's two older sisters were rummaging through her closet and personal things. When they sensed my presence, they turned in surprise with a frightened look on their faces. One of them nervously said, "Oh, do you want any of these things, dear? They probably won't fit you anyway, and surely a young girl like you would not want a mink coat living in Southern California, now would you?" I never cared for either one of them, even before this. They reeked of greed and snobbery, their behavior was really no surprise, just a confirmation.

It took me over ten years before I could talk about the death of my mother, because the pain was so great. I am so thankful for what God has done in my life. Jesus Christ has brought complete healing, restoration, and deliverance to my soul. God is no respecter of persons. What He has done for me, He will do for you. Believe in the finished work of the cross and trust Him with your whole heart.

> *The Lord is my shepherd, I shall not want.*
> *He makes me lie down in green pastures; He*
> *leads me beside quiet waters. He restores my*
> *soul;; He guides me in the paths of righteous-*
> *ness for His name's sake.*   (Psalms 23:1-3)

Maybe there are some wounded areas in your heart that you are not consciously aware of, because they have been so thoroughly buried, and thereby have wounded the deepest parts of your soul. You can ask the Holy Spirit to begin revealing any areas that could be hindering you, thus quenching God's best plan for your life. He is our Healer; He longs to bring healing and wholeness to you, as only a loving, Heavenly Father can.

I loved my mother so very much, despite her alcoholism. God gave me such compassion at a very young age for her. I never remember blaming her for what our life was like. I just recall feeling sorry for her and desperately wishing that I could help her.

> **None of the things this world can offer will ever be able to give us everlasting happiness.**

None of the things this world can offer will ever be able to give us everlasting happiness or joy, which my mother eventually came to realize. It's not found in money, alcohol, drugs, multiple spouses, or anything else. Joy is a gift that comes from God, and from Him alone. He can fill every void or vacuum in your heart.

A few years have passed...

We were in upstate New York, where my husband felt God had called him to plant a church. One Sunday morning, we had a particular guest preacher who was recommended by another pastor who said, "This is a man graced with humility and he carries a very strong prophetic anointing. I think you will find that he will be a blessing to your congregation." My husband said, "Yes" to having him come and minister.

After he finished preaching the Word of God, he called for those who wanted prayer to come to the altar. I quickly ran up to be right in line with the rest. I never turn down an opportunity to receive prayer, especially when it comes from an anointed vessel of God.

I had very little exposure to the prophetic at that time, however, I knew this minister moved in that anointing. When he came to me and prayed, he said:

"You are not to worry, and you are to put your mind at rest; your mother is in heaven."

I was dumbfounded. I did not know this minister and he did not know me, my husband, or anyone else in my family. Nor did he did know if my mother was alive or dead!

But God knew...

My heart was encouraged, and I wept.

Like apples of gold in settings of silver is a word spoken in right circumstances.
(Proverbs 25:11)

I believe before my mother breathed her last breath, she may have said something like the thief on the cross who pled, "Jesus, remember me when You come into Your kingdom." And what was Jesus' answer to him in Luke's account?

"Truly I say to you, today you shall be with Me in Paradise." (Luke 23:42-43)

❦

Chapter 5

The Glitter of Vegas Soon Ended
~ Married Life Began ~

*O*ur honeymoon was officially over. We had so much fun spending the wedding money my parents gave us like drunken sailors. We lived like the rich and famous for one week, but after that we went back to the real world, not the Las Vegas world. Married life in Los Angeles slowly became a reality.

Al made me laugh so much, and I was falling more and more in love with him each and every day. The Lord knew that He was just what I needed, for I tended to be so serious. We were exact opposites. He had the gift of making almost anyone laugh, and his high school teachers said that he should be a comedian.

New research indicates why laughter may be the best pain medicine. They are just now catching up with what the Lord knew all along. Laughing with friends, watching funny movies, etc., releases feel-good, brain chemicals called endorphins, which also relieve pain.

A merry heart doeth good like a medicine.
(Proverbs 17:22 KJV)

SETTLING IN...

When we arrived back at his apartment (which then became our apartment), his roommate was still there, even though he was told earlier that he had to leave. So, he moved back in with his parents.

Unexpectedly, Al's cousin and his cousin's friend from Connecticut showed up at our doorstep just two days after we arrived home. He did not know that Al had just gotten married. The next morning, I asked them what they wanted for breakfast and they said, "Scrambled eggs." I got frantic because I realized all of a sudden that I did not know how to make scrambled eggs. So, the three men decided they would show me how it was done. Our uninvited visitors were probably thinking, "What kind of a girl did Al marry? She does not even know how to make scrambled eggs." I never could have imagined at that time that eventually cooking would become one of the loves of my life, and a wonderful gift that God graciously gave me.

Back from our honeymoon, standing in front of my parents' home

Finally, Al called his mother, and it probably took more courage than I could wrap my brain around at this early stage of our marriage. Stella was known to have the ability to sometimes reduce the strongest, most astute, and self-confident person to a speechless, babbling, human being; all the while leaving the person in her presence with nothing left but to simply ponder what in the world just happened. She was a very strong woman, "large and in charge," who liked to be in control of everyone and everything. She was living in San Francisco with her new husband of one year, leaving her son, a senior in high school, alone in the apartment. My husband said he had fervently prayed that God would find his mother a husband. When the husband appeared, he said he then knew for sure there was a God, a God who

Left to right: father-in-law, mother-in-law (Stella), my mother, and stepfather.

answered prayer! It was another seven years before he gave his life to Christ.

HELP! I WANT TO FLY AWAY!

About one week after being back from our honeymoon, we had what I like to call, "The Unforgettable Lunch."

Crying mothers… one docile and inebriated, the other bossy and controlling. This was the scenario of our "Meet the Parents Lunch."

"Oh, that I had the wings of a dove. Could someone or something please, just p-l-e-a-s-e, beam me out of here!" Al told me that his mother, Stella, didn't like to be called "Mom." She preferred to be called Stella by her sons. That should give you your first clue.

> *Oh, that I had wings like a dove! I would fly away and be at rest. Behold, I would wander far away, I would lodge in the wilderness.*
>
> (Psalms 55:6-7)

The mothers wore yellow dresses, and the two stepfathers were sporting identical seersucker suits. It really was quite a sight! It certainly was not planned, but it was amusing, if nothing else.

This was the first time both sets of parents had met. My new husband and I were the topic of what I perceived to be a dreadful gathering.

The fact that Stella had to find out from Al's roommate that her son had eloped to Las Vegas was awkward to say the least. That was another "happy" discussion at our little lunch.

I didn't know what was flowing more frequently at that point, the tears or the cocktails. Of course, by the end of the lunch at the country club, everyone was pretty well soused, "drunk as skunks" to be more exact, with the exception of my new husband, my new mother-in-law, and me.

Any worries the four of them had in the beginning were glossed over by the numbing effects of alcohol. Their spoken worries and shared concerns about their children's future seemed to pass, if only momentarily.

FATHER DOVE

Father Dove and me

After we were married a few months, I became a pitiful, Catholic convert. I felt we needed some "religion" since we were soon to be parents. My mother was Episcopalian, but never went to church. When I was seven years old, my paternal grandparents took me to the Presbyterian church where I memorized the 23rd Psalm. Stella sent my husband to Catholic mass, where he was an altar boy. Eventually, the priest caught him tasting some of the communion wine, which abruptly ended his duties in the church. He stopped going after that and went to the corner store instead with the fifty cents his mother gave him for church. He used the money for the pinball machine and candy. Stella would ask her friends who went to mass if they saw her son, Jerry (aka Al). There were too many "Als" in the family, so she called him by his middle name. He never did go back to church. Later in life when he told his mother, she said, "I knew something was fishy. None of my friends ever saw you at any mass," and they both laughed.

Over a decade later, when my husband told her that he was going to be a pastor, she was devastated. She was the youngest of twelve children and called some of her siblings that were still alive to tell them the news, I guess to be consoled. They told her, "Stella, didn't we always pray for a **"God, can't I just go directly to You?"** priest in the family?" She said, "Yes." They replied, "Well, this is the next best thing!" That seemed to settle the issue for her.

Anyway, wanting so much to be a good mother, I took the Catholic lessons. However, I would get rattled in confession, forget the prayers, and ended up making stuff up that I never did. It was nothing short of ridiculous. I couldn't be a hypocrite. I didn't like to eat fish on Fridays, and there were other things I found hard to reconcile within my own heart.

My thoughts were, "God, can't I just go directly to You? You are greater than the priest, the pastor, and the prophet! You are the President, so to speak. You are the CEO of the world. I will go to You!" I loved Father Dove, the priest who was so understanding and quite liberal for the times. He said,

"Not to worry, you don't have to have a zillion children, and don't worry about the Friday fish thing either."

Please let the reader understand that this is not a slam in any way, shape, or form to beautiful Catholics everywhere. It was just the way I perceived some church traditions and the way the Holy Spirit was leading me at the time. Years later, when I was teaching a ladies Bible study in our non-denominational church, one of the ladies said, "I'm Catholic, so you ladies probably don't understand," thinking she was the only one. I felt prompted to ask the question, "How many Catholics do we have in here?" Ninety percent of the women raised their hands! One day, when we will all meet God face-to-face, I don't think He will care whether we are Baptists, Catholics, Lutherans, Presbyterians, or any other denominations. The most important issue is whether or not we have truly received Jesus as Lord of our lives. Besides, God always looks at the heart.

SURPRISE!

Yep, it really shouldn't have been a surprise at all, since my husband and I had been jumping up-and-down on the bed having pillow fights like little kids. You really should not do that when you are seven and a half months pregnant. No kidding. We had so much fun! Maybe our parents were right when they said, "Kids having kids."

That same evening, while sitting at the dining room table, my water broke! My husband was so nervous, frantically riffling through our little address book trying to find the OB/GYN's number. When he finally got the doctor on the line, he blurted out, "This is Sallie, Al's husband!" He was a wreck! Fear and anxiety were beginning to grip my heart, and I said to my husband, "Please ask him if he has ever delivered any little babies before?"

The doctor put me on strict bed rest which lasted for about two weeks before the first labor pains emerged. You did not know the sex of your child in those days until they were born. The air of expectancy and excitement could be felt in the labor and delivery room as we anxiously awaited the announcement of the sex of our soon-to-be newborn baby. The birth could not come soon enough, as I had already been in intense labor for forty-eight hours.

Our daughter was born one month early, weighing only four pounds. I can't begin to tell you the great joy we both

> **Our daughter was born one month early, weighing only four pounds.**

experienced upon seeing this precious, little baby right after she was born. It was love at first sight! The Lord knew from the beginning of time the desires of our hearts. He also knew how much we both longed for a happy family. Having started a family of our own, we were "over the top" thrilled to be new parents.

While I was in the hospital, Al took the second bedroom of our small apartment, painting and decorating it, until it turned into what I thought was the most beautiful nursery in the whole world. It was magically turned into a very colorful, whimsical room. He managed to do all of this with limited funds. I was so impressed and loved him all the more. I slowly began to realize what a tender, sensitive heart was in this man that I married just a few short months before.

As I slowly walked into the room for the first time after leaving the hospital, I was able to see the wonderful surprise my husband had waiting for me. I was overwhelmed and speechless, tears began to flow like a waterfall down my hot cheeks.

LOBSTER CLAW

After several years of marriage, I started to develop a very painful eczema type of rash on my right hand that would crack and bleed. It only came around the Christmas season. We finally put two and two together. Looking at previous pictures helped us realize that it only occurred at that time of year. My right hand would swell up and turn bright red resembling a large lobster claw. It only "showed up" when Stella "showed up" to stay with us!

The cause? STRESS! She made me a nervous wreck!

One year while visiting us, she got in a snit about something that I can't even remember. She said she was flying back to San Francisco. No one stopped her. When she called later speaking sheepishly to my husband, he was very firm with her. I think this time he actually called her "Mom." He said, "Mom, you are not welcome back here until you give my wife an apology. My wife is the sweetest, kindest woman I have ever met and you owe her an apology!" As I look back, I am very thankful that early on in our marriage, he set a strong boundary with his mother, in a very loving but firm and matter-of-fact manner.

We all laughed about it years later and so did Stella. My husband, every now and then, would say to her in a joking manner, "Remember when you made my wife's hand crack and bleed?" I certainly don't put the responsibility on her. I was not capable, at that time in my life, to set my own boundaries with her. I allowed the stress which manifested in my physical body. At the end of her life, she called me the daughter she never had. God did an amazing work in me over many decades to get to that point.

THE ENTREPRENEUR

Al was a hairstylist by trade, and when our first daughter was about a year old, he purchased the salon in West Los Angeles where he was working. The owner wanted to retire. We thought it was perfect!

One of his employees, Nora Lee, was always talking to him about the Lord. He really did not want to hear anything about what she had to say on the matter. When he would voice his concerns regarding the business, she would always say to him, "God will take care of it; He loves you." Whenever the opportunity arose, she would always weave the goodness of the Lord and His amazing love into the conversation.

Looking back, I am so thankful for her boldness and burden for him. Only God knew how lost we both were.

What really stood out was her persistence. Al had plenty himself, but her sweet spirit in the face of his rejection touched his heart. She was not deterred in the least and continued to talk about the Lord and pray for my husband.

Every year around Christmas, we would open our home for the employees. Many brought us house gifts, but Nora Lee brought me a book entitled *The Christian Home*. I must tell you that my first reaction was that this was a very presumptive gift! She was presuming that I was a Christian. I know that it was because of her sensitivity and obedience to the Holy Spirit.

When everyone left our Christmas party that evening, I promptly put away the book, never intending to read any of it. After all, I was liberal-minded, and I thought Christians were narrow-minded bigots. I worried about all the other religions. What about them? Some of them prayed three or four times a day. They did so much of what I thought were holy things. One thing I knew for sure, I was anything but holy according to those standards.

The call came the next day that the salon was in flames. When the building was closed, the boutique portion of the salon suddenly caught fire causing extensive damage.

Thankfully, no one was in the building at the time. The damage was mostly contained in the area that was sectioned off for a ladies' dress boutique. This seemed like a natural fit for a salon that catered mostly to Jewish ladies living in the area, who loved getting their hair done several times a week, and we loved having them.

Down the street from the salon, my husband rented another building that would be used entirely for the dress boutique. We named the business " 3 Plus 1." The name was given because there were three of us in our little family at that time, and I was pregnant with our second daughter.

One year earlier, I lost a son in my seventh month of pregnancy. This was the result of a condition called placenta previa which caused copious amounts of blood clots emitting from my body, the size of small grapefruits according to the nurse's description.

The nurses on the floor where I was staying seemed completely disinterested in their patients. Day after day, right outside the door of my room (which by the way had been my home for the last month), I could smell cigarette smoke wafting through my door. The nurse's voices were unusually loud, and I could clearly hear them gossiping in the background about all the hospital drama relating to employees, as to "whose doing what with whom." Good grief! That was the least of my concerns!

My call light would be on for what seemed like forever and a day before anyone noticed or bothered to come into my room. I was not allowed to get out of bed for any reason, so obviously I was completely dependent on their assistance.

*Nursing school graduation: top left to right, daughter Carrie, me, and Al.
Bottom: daughter Kelli, cousins Dennis and David*

I always believed that nurses were supposed to be "angels of mercy." Well, they certainly did not act like angels, at least not on that particular hospital floor, for sure! That experience alone made me decide later to go back to school and finish my education to eventually become an RN.

Nursing school graduation

If anyone had told me that one day, I would become an RN, I would not have believed it. I could barely cut up a raw chicken when we got married, much less a dead cat in a biology lab. What I did not realize initially was that I would have to take a course in chemistry. After finding this out, I wanted to quit. Chemistry to me was like taking a class on rocket science. I did not know how I could possibly ever get through that course. So, I told my fellow nursing student that our first test in chemistry was going to be a confirmation if I was even to pursue this nursing career. My husband continually encouraged me, saying that he knew I could do it. I studied, but I did not really understand most of it. The day of the first test I silently prayed, "Lord, this is in Your hands and it will be a sign to me if I am to continue in nursing." I told my girlfriend, who

> **If anyone had told me that one day, I would become an RN, I would not have believed it.**

was taking the same test, that I did not think I did very well. Turns out, I got the highest grade in the class! There were three more tests, and I ended up getting a B in chemistry, which was nothing short of a miracle. My friend said, "I thought you told me you were not going to do well." I said, "Yes, I did say that, but it was all God, for sure." When it was time to take the state boards, which were several months after graduation, I cried out to the Lord again the night before the testing. He answered me so clearly from Isaiah 66:9: "Shall I bring to the point of birth and not give delivery? says the Lord." I immediately knew that God had this, and I was going to do just fine. I went to sleep with a grateful heart and woke up the next morning knowing that all was well.

The Catholic hospital that I was in saved the babies first, so they told my husband that I was probably going to die, and that he should be prepared for the worst. Because I pleaded with them to let me go home after being stuck there for almost an entire month, they finally released me, making sure I had 24/7 help. They discharged me on Good Friday. On Easter Sunday, I went into labor, and immediately was taken back to the hospital where our son was born. He lived only a few hours. I'm sorry I did not turn to look at him, because the doctors told me ahead of time that he probably would not survive, and if he did, he would be a vegetable. I felt numb again and so sad. At the time, I just couldn't bear to look at him. My husband later said he was beautiful and looked a lot like our firstborn. Several days later, we had a small burial service with just my husband and me at a Catholic cemetery. We named our son Anthony.

RIGHT TIMING IS EVERYTHING!

Three Plus One was written on the lovely sign above our new building that would house beautiful, original dresses. Al contracted the lady who had made dresses for our boutique in the salon, and that is how it developed into a small business of manufacturing ladies' dresses. The hair salon was still in full operation several doors up the street.

The problem with the dresses was the timing. The 60s were tumultuous, and it seemed as if the culture we had known started to drastically change. Ladies were not wearing dresses anymore or even bras for that matter. The nation was changing rapidly with the Vietnam War protesters showing up everywhere and deserters leaving the country. There were the Watts, the Los Angeles race riots (sometimes referred to as the Watts Rebellion that took place in the Watts neighborhood of Los Angeles), and many other changes bombarding our nation. The hippie generation was in full swing, with topless shoeshine girls showing up in the large cities, particularly prevalent in San Francisco.

Three Plus One

Albert Yusko shown here in front of his new store, 3 Plus 1 Manufacturing Company, opens an outlet this month for his women's wear manufacturing company. Albert is well known to the women of the area through his beauty salon Empress Coiffeurs With Boutique Shop.

Al in front of the "3 Plus 1"
manufacturing company he started in 1969

Around this time, my husband met a former schoolteacher. He told him about a business opportunity that promised a tremendous income. He then, as proof, pulled out copies of large checks to show him. My husband was ripe for change, being tired of all the smog alerts and earthquakes and got on board with a multi-level, oil additive company. He became so successful that we ended up driving to New York where he opened the tri-state area for them.

Chapter 6

The Greatest is Love

When we finally arrived in New York, I started unpacking my cookbooks and noticed that the book given to me by Nora Lee on *The Christian Home* had been inadvertently put with the others. I certainly would not have taken it with me! We left almost everything we owned in California, renting our home, fully intending to return one day. We took only the bare necessities with us. I love to cook, so for me, taking my cookbooks was a necessity.

I am eternally grateful for people who never give up, even in the face of ridicule and persecution for their faith. I don't know where Nora Lee is to this day. She has no idea that when my husband and I left California to live in New York, we came to know Christ as our Savior and later became ordained ministers of the gospel, pastoring for many decades.

.CIGARETTES AND THE CLEANERS

"JESUS!" came the LOUD answer from the girl behind the counter.

Her strong, confident voice blasted me while I was dropping off my dry cleaning. What kind of an answer was that? "No wonder this poor girl is not married," I thought. You can't go around telling people things like that. They will think you are a "looney tune" or a religious fanatic!

All I said was, "I am struggling with trying to quit smoking," and then I asked her the simple question, "How did you quit?" I would have never expected the response I got! She simply shared how she was able to "kick the habit" and become totally free from any nicotine addiction. It was Jesus!

Well that did it for me…I was out of there! God only knows what she would have preached about next.

I was heavily addicted to cigarettes from the age of thirteen (blowing smoke rings was probably the only thing I learned how to do in boarding school besides playing tennis). By the time I was twenty-seven years of age, I was smoking three packs a day, along with little cigars called cigarillos. Some people are able to quit by sheer will power, but that was not the case with me. I could not take a shower without lighting a cigarette, resting it on the bathroom sink, and taking drags off and on. I know what you're thinking, and you are right… it was pitiful! Addiction is a terrible thing, no matter what the addiction might be.

Cigarettes and cigarette machines were everywhere you turned. I really didn't know anyone who didn't smoke in those days. My mother used to buy my cigarettes for me at thirteen. You could smoke almost anywhere, and this was before any of the serious health warnings were issued. There were even magazine ads saying, "Smoke Lucky Strikes; they are good for your health."

After going to another dry cleaner for a few months, I finally came back to the original one where Roseanne, the "Jesus girl," worked. It was closer to home and it was a much better dry cleaner. My husband was wearing suits and ties seven days a week, teaching and training sales reps for the oil additive company. My mother-in-law always said we should have owned and operated a dry cleaner, for the amount of business we gave them. I think she probably frequented the cleaner once or twice a year at best. I would sometimes take his clothes in three or four times a week. He worked every day and most evenings, making lots of money, and was very "full of himself," I must say. We laugh about it now. We were both so lost and far from God.

Roseanne and I would have brief conversations as I continued to come in week after week, and she would say to me, "You know, I have a book you might like to read called *The Greatest is Love.* I will bring it to you." The problem was, she always forgot it. This annoyed me. Why was she always forgetting to bring me this book? After all, she had recommended it.

We were both so lost and far from God.

I love to read and was anxious to get my hands on it. But, yes! That was a good thing! God knows all about our natures, everything about us.

> *O Lord, You have searched me and known me. You know when I sit down and when I rise up; You understand my thought from afar. You scrutinize my path and my lying down, and are intimately acquainted with all my ways. Even before there is a word on my tongue, behold, O Lord, You know it all.*
>
> (Psalms 139:1-4)

He knew if I ever suspected that she was "pushing" this book or if I knew it was a Bible, I would NEVER read it. I had plenty of Bibles at home, and they never interested me. If I did pick one up, I always started in the beginning and the particular translation we owned was not relevant to me, nor did it seem interesting.

She finally brought "the book." It was a paperback with a blue cover, showing a dad carrying a little child on his shoulders. Not even a hint whatsoever that it was a Bible, when in fact, it was a New Testament, in an easy-to-read, modern translation.

Once I picked it up and started reading, I could not put it down. The more I read, the more my heart would pound. The Spirit of God was wooing me, and I did not comprehend all that was transpiring on the inside of me. I just knew that this was the most wonderful book I had ever read.

I knew my husband would NEVER be interested in any of this, for sure! We never talked about God or religion per se, and he seemed only to be interested in making money and providing a nice living for his family.

Fear began to grip my heart…I began thinking of all the "what ifs." I had thoughts like, "maybe my husband will divorce me," as I knew in my heart that our life and lifestyle was getting ready to radically change from anything we had ever experienced before.

The only time we talked about religion was after we were married. We exchanged vows at the Justice of the Peace in Las

The paperback New Testament that was given to me from Roseanne in the cleaners

Vegas, Nevada. My mother-in-law, Stella, wanted us to get remarried in the Catholic Church, which was okay with me since I didn't really adhere to any religion.

Sitting at the kitchen table while reading this New Testament, with cigarettes and an ashtray close by, I remembered what Roseanne had said to me in the cleaners about how Jesus helped her to quit smoking.

I hated the addiction so much and wanted more than anything to quit but was never able to do so without starting back up again, So I said a prayer: "God, if you can take these cigarettes from me that would be beyond wonderful." This was not even a "prayer of faith." I didn't really believe it. I wasn't sure if it was going to happen, or if God even heard me.

The exact moment my prayer ended, my hand that was holding the cigarette froze! I could not bring that cigarette up to my mouth, period. I put the cigarette out in the ash-tray, still trying to comprehend what had just taken place. From that day on, and to this present day, decades later, I am still in awe of God's good-

> **The exact moment my prayer ended, my hand that was holding the cigarette froze!**

ness, that in our moments of unbelief and arrogance, He will show up demonstrating His loving kindness and grace.

We ended up going to "Roseanne from the cleaners" church, whose young pastor's name was Tom Hatcher. He was a recent transplant from California. How about that? God knew just who to place in my life. I was so hungry. I had a million questions, and he patiently and lovingly answered them all.

When Pastor Hatcher came to our home to talk to me about baptism, we did not realize that my husband was intently listening to every word the pastor was sharing about baptism and salvation. All that while, the Holy Spirit was touching his heart. The Bible says that if any of your husbands are disobedient to the word, they may be won without a word, by the behavior of their wives. I did not know I was being scriptural at the time. I just didn't say anything because I did not think my husband was interested or that God could save him. Al said that if I had "preached" to him, he might not have come to the Lord when he did. Because I was quiet, and he was able to see a change in me, the Holy Spirit was able to work on his heart.

Later, after we had been Christians for a while, I was not so silent. I felt the Holy Spirit needed my help in dealing with my husband. A wise woman, the wife of an evangelist we knew, told me she prays like this for her husband: "God, you are my husband's boss. You deal with him and speak to him." Wise words indeed. I was learning to pray more and be silent when needed. I am not talking about being a doormat or never speaking up, but our husbands do not need sermons from their wives on the Word. It is a process and I failed many times. However, I

> **I was learning to pray more and be silent when needed.**

never felt condemned by the Lord. I trusted that He knew my heart—that I intended to always listen to that still, small voice and by His grace, yield and obey.

I am forever grateful to God for bringing Pastor Tom Hatcher across our path. He led Al and I both to Christ, and we were baptized together by immersion. Pastor Hatcher became our best friend, To this present day, he remains a precious gift to us. Some years later, he moved from New York back to California. He was very instrumental in playing a huge role in each of our lives as we began our new life in Christ. Our walk with the Lord, from that moment in time up to this day, has been anything but boring!

We love you, Pastor Tom Hatcher! Thank you for giving to the Lord. We are two lives that were changed.

See, you just never know whose lives you are touching, even when you think you are not making a difference.

You may never realize, on this side of heaven, the enormous influence you have on someone else's life. My encouragement to the reader would be to stay faithful. In the end, we will see everything clearly, just as we have been clearly seen.

> *For now we see in a mirror dimly, but then face to face; now I know in part, but then I will know fully just as I also have been fully known.* (1 Corinthians 13:12)

Chapter 7

The Journey

"What next, Lord?" I thought after the amazing cigarette miracle. Watching my hand freeze in midair so as not to be able to take a drag was pretty astonishing. So naturally, I thought everything was going to be that easy and quick.

Shortly thereafter, Al finally got a night off work and was able to go to a Bible study with me in the home of a wonderful, Norwegian couple, Kaare and Helen Titland.

It was there where we heard a color-blind, chalkboard artist, Phil Saint. Phil was one of the amazing saints whose brother, Nate, was a missionary pilot to Ecuador and was martyred by the Auca Indians (documented in the book, *Through Gates of Splendor* and the movie, *End of the Spear*). He was accompanied by four others, and they willingly laid their lives down, as they had long, shafted spears hurled at them for the sake of the gospel. Al listened intently to Nate speak and draw on the chalkboard the salvation message. The Spirit of God was wooing him, and when the pastor came to our home a week later to talk to me about baptism by immersion, Al asked the pastor to bring a baptismal robe for him as well. He wanted to be baptized! The following Sunday, we were baptized together. Then, the real journey began in the Lord.

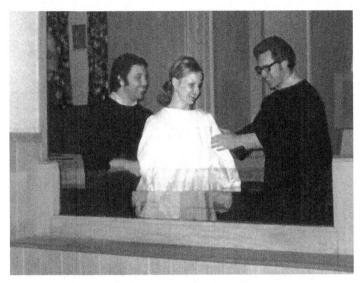

My husband and me being baptized by Pastor Tom Hatcher in 1972

Remember I said my husband was working day and night, making lots of money. Well soon after this, the company he worked for was defunct and the CEO was put in jail.

From fancy cars to frumpy cars so quickly. How could this be? There was a popular book out at the time, *How to Live Like a King's Kid*, and it was hard to understand why everything in our life started to go south. After all, we had just come to the Lord, and this was not our interpretation of living like "king's kids." Before this, we were living "high on the hog," according to the world's standards.

At that point, the car I drove had so many spots on it, it looked like it had chickenpox. One day, when my husband and I were driving up the New York State Thruway, I decided to take a poll of all the cars we passed, and tears started flowing down my face. When my husband asked what was wrong, I blurted out, "I noticed there was not one car on the entire thruway uglier than mine." I was feeling sorry for myself. I

I soon realized God was more interested in my character than in my circumstances.

soon realized God was more interested in my character than in my circumstances. Later repenting of all self-pity, I felt so completely free. At that point, I really didn't care what kind of a car I drove, or if I even had a car. I was truly thankful for having a vehicle and for learning such valuable lessons of trust and contentment in all things. My heart was settled and at complete peace.

About a month later, my husband comes bursting through our front door and says, "Sallie, I just got you another car." I said, "What?" I had just started to really like the car I had, chickenpox and all! The poor guy was dumbfounded. That's why God wants husbands to live with their wives in an understanding way. Anyway, he told me that someone he had previously worked with was selling his Ford, and he would sell it to him for an unbelievably low price. It was a used car, but to me it might as well had been a Rolls-Royce.

"He Really Didn't Say That, Did He?"

I remember one Thanksgiving season, when I was studying for finals in nursing school, that my husband asked the pastor if he could make an announcement from the pulpit, and the pastor said, "Yes." Well, unknown to me, my husband invited anyone who did not have a place to go for Thanksgiving dinner to come to our home for a Thanksgiving meal. I said to myself, "He really didn't just say that, did he? He's got to be kidding." The initial thought of not knowing who or what would show up seemed overwhelming at first, especially with my nursing finals around the corner. What I did not know at the time was that this would become the forerunner of a ministry that would reach the poor and feed the hungry at New Hope Gospel Fellowship, in Schenectady, New York. No paper plates: our china, crystal, and silver were used because I wanted it to be no different than what I would do for my friends or family. We ended up with around fifteen extra people, and there was more than enough for all. I also ended up having a lot of extra time to study for my finals. The Lord was showing me once again, when we put His agenda first, He adds all these things to us. Everyone pitched in with the cleanup, and it was a glorious Thanksgiving. The Presence of the Lord was everywhere. All who came just could not thank us enough, while expressing that it was the best Thanksgiving they ever had. All the glory and praise to our great God!

God knew just what we both needed to begin forming us into His image. He was teaching us, equipping us for everything that would be needed up ahead for this awe-inspiring journey. We both needed a lot of work, and He wasted no time in starting our training.

> **God knew just what we both needed to begin forming us into His image.**

The home we bought, after we lived in the rented house, was on the verge of being repossessed. However, through some miraculous circumstances, we were able to keep the house. Our finances were scarce, but through it all, we learned to trust God in a way that I never thought would have been possible.

My prayer life was increasing and growing stronger every day. One of the many reasons was that my car needed prayer every morning for it to just start.

Not that I speak from want, for I have learned to be content in whatever circumstances I am. I know how to get along with humble means, and I also know how to live in prosperity; in any and every circumstance I have learned the secret of being filled and going hungry, both of having abundance and suffering need. I can do all things through Him who strengthens me.
(Philippians 4:11-13)

A New Day Was Dawning

It was during this time of great financial setbacks that the Lord gave Al the vision for starting what would quickly become a very successful, natural, henna hair care company. The company distributed henna products, cosmetics, and vitamins nationally and internationally. Al was given a vision by the Lord to develop henna hair care products in dozens of shades, when there were only three or four shades on the market at the time. The Lord wastes nothing and used Al's beauty background in formulating and developing these various colors

The Lord gave him great wisdom in marketing and radical favor within the industry, making our company number one in the health food industry for henna hair coloring. The business grew rapidly, and the favor of God was evident everywhere. God continued to bless the business above our wildest dreams, far beyond what we could have possibly imagined. The days of meager finances were a faint memory.

Owning his own business gave him the flexibility to be able to go to Bible school. His heart was always for the Lord and he was always at church serving in whatever capacity he could.

While my husband was spending a great deal of his time serving the Lord and the church, the business was flourishing. He continued to seek God and His Kingdom FIRST, and the Lord kept increasing and blessing the business and adding all these things to us.

> *"But seek first His kingdom and His righteousness, and all these things will be added to you."*　　　　　　(Matthew 6:33)

But still, there was an unsettling…a stirring in Al's spirit. He knew deep down that God was calling him to full-time ministry.

"Who would ever live in Schenectady?" Those were my exact words as we drove up the New York State Thruway on our way to Lake Placid for our annual ski trip.

Be careful what you say. You may have to "eat those words" one day. Never in a million years did I think we would live there! You could smell the pepperoni pizza coming up the thruway.

Heavy torrents of rain raced wildly down our windshield, making it difficult to hear anything else. We were sitting in our car waiting to get gas. Those were the days when a service attendant actually filled your tank.

Suddenly, I turned and saw tears streaming down my husband's face. His voice choked and cracked. Words, ever so slowly, rolling off his tongue.

"I really believe that God is calling me into full-time ministry, as a pastor."

You could hear a pin drop at this point. The heavy rain had abruptly ceased as quickly as it had started. We were staring intently at each other. After a few moments, which seemed like an eternity, I said, "If God is calling you, you better listen and obey Him."

A few short months passed…and before I knew it, we were in our car with the kids, the dog, and my mother-in-law, Stella, driving to Schenectady.

What an adventure!

Terrified…it was all beginning to slowly sink in.

We left the business in the hands of a faithful, longtime employee, or at least so we thought. Within less than a year, she stole the company along with one of our salesmen, moving the operation to a different state and changing the name. Not long after that, the entire company went defunct. After finding this out, my husband asked the employee how she could possibly do such a thing when over the years she was treated like family, along with being handsomely compensated for her work. Her reply was, "Well, Al, business is business." Greed and jealousy seemed to overrule any reasoning, and so she and her partner felt justified in their own eyes, since we began living in Upstate

New York doing full time ministry. The irony was, we could have possibly sold the company to Revlon, for they had been taking a serious look at acquiring this lucrative business we decided not to sell.

It was so hurtful, yet at the same time, we knew we had to forgive them if we were ever to move forward. Forgiving is not so much about those who have wronged you, it is for you. Keep in mind that forgiving is not forgetting, it is simply remembering without anger. It frees you up to heal your body and soul, which is your mind, will, and emotions. Forgiveness is taking the high road, and it opens a new pathway of peace, helping you go on despite what has happened. We knew we had to forgive. We also knew in our hearts that God did not want us to fall back on anything but Him. He is our Provider, not our business, job, family, or anything else.

I said, "Lord, I don't know what a pastor's wife is supposed to do, and besides that, I don't even play the piano or teach. You know I am very shy. You know this Lord!" He really didn't seem to be fazed one bit by my excuses.

"I know what I will do," I thought at last…"I will listen to Christian television. Maybe I can learn what I am supposed to do as a pastor's wife!" We went out and purchased a big TV, and unknown to me, we were the only street in the entire neighborhood that could not get cable where the shows aired. "Oh God," I screamed in my heart, "This is terrible! These people pray so eloquently and seem to know a thousand times

Do you ever feel like God is not listening and is not concerned?

more than I know. God; you know I need help."

Silence, once again.

Do you ever feel like God is not listening and is not concerned?

The fourth chapter of Exodus kept whirling around in my head. When I read it, I knew the Lord had spoken to me through what He spoke to Moses.

> *The Lord said to him, "Who has made*
> *man's mouth? Or who makes him mute or*
> *deaf, or seeing or blind? Is it not I, the Lord?*
> *Now then go, and I, even I, will be with your*
> *mouth, and teach you what you are to say."*
> (Exodus 4:11-12)

One morning, I woke up from a very unusual dream. In the dream, I just could not get enough water, no matter how much I drank. I would drink and drink and drink and still be thirsty! Upon awakening, I pondered this, and my nursing mindset kicked in. I thought, "Am I getting diabetes?" What was the meaning of that dream?

Almost immediately, my hunger and thirst for the Word of God seemed unquenchable. I just could not get enough. I devoured everything in the Bible. The Holy Spirit started to teach me great and wondrous things that I had not seen before. It became clear to me what this dream had meant. God indeed heard my prayer for HELP. He did not want me duplicating or modeling anything that I thought I was supposed to do or be from Christian television or anyone else for that matter. The Lord is the potter and we are the clay. He wants to shape each one of us individually into His likeness, for His purposes and His glory.

> *"Call to Me and I will answer you, and I*
> *will tell you great and mighty things, which*
> *you do not know."* (Jeremiah 33:3)

Several years had passed by and we were finally able to get cable. When I turned on the Christian station for the first time, I was shocked and disheartened by what I saw. It seemed as if men and their ministries were elevated to such pomp and grandeur that it grieved me. Shortly after that, several of these so-called ministries came to their demise. Very sad indeed, especially for those who put their total trust in them, elevating them to a position that should have been God's and His alone. The tragic result of all of this was that many stopped serving the Lord. At that time, it became clearer than ever, God did not want me to emulate any of these ministries. He wanted me to be taught by Him alone, for which I am forever grateful. God does not want carbon copies.

One Sunday morning, during our church service in Schenectady, we had a guest evangelist who ministered in the prophetic. When it was time for him to pray for me, he said, "You are going to be bold and strong and teach women."

Well, I started to laugh. I really thought this prophet was confused and that he had laid his hand on the wrong person. "My husband standing next to me was the one he probably meant," I mused.

God knew how shy I was, so much so that when I gave my heart to Christ, the pastor asked me to give a brief testimony and I was too timid to do so. The Lord also knew that I didn't even care for most women. I thought, "What kind of word had I received?"

God knows what He has put in YOU, even if you don't know yourself!

Surely, as the prophet had spoken, it has all come to pass just as he said. I became bold in the Lord and started teaching women and actually loving it and the women to whom I ministered.

THE CALL

It was 5 a.m. on a weekday when I heard a loud and clear voice call my name, "Sallie!" I looked around my bedroom. My husband was sound asleep. So were our two, young children down the hall. I thought I must have imagined it and turned over to go back to sleep. Suddenly, I heard for the second time in the same clear, loud voice, "Sallie!" This should have caused the whole household to wake up, yet everyone was still asleep. I then realized that it was the Lord calling me. I had never heard an audible voice before, nor have I since that day, so I knew it was the Lord calling my name. I sat straight up in bed and got up! I had been telling the Lord for weeks that I wanted to get up earlier and spend some time with Him before everyone woke up. After they did, I always got so busy getting my children ready to go to school. Then one thing led to another and pretty soon, the day was gone before I knew it even started. I prayed previously that I would get up earlier, but my flesh was weak. I loved my fluffy, little bed with all the pillows, and it was hard for me to get up most mornings. I have been getting up very early most of the time ever since. The Lord knew that He wanted me to separate myself, and set aside time each day for Him. He wanted me to know Him more intimately and to learn of His great plans for my life. Our fellowship with one another became all together lovely, rich, and very fragrant. There is no better friend than Jesus.

> *"For I know the plans I have for you, de-*
> *clares the Lord, plans to prosper you and not*
> *to harm you, plans to give you hope and a*
> *future."*   (Jeremiah 29:11 NIV)

BAPTISM OF THE HOLY SPIRIT AND FIRE

After coming to faith in Christ, I was invited to a lunch at the home of one of the three elderly ladies in our church. I had been seeking the gift of tongues for several months, but never received the manifestation. This particular day, after we finished our lunch, the nice ladies put me on a chair in the middle of the living room and said they wanted to pray for me. Next thing I knew, these ladies were laying their hands on me and praying fervently. But before they started, they explained the gift of speaking in tongues. They said the gift was like a present and I was to untie the ribbon and open it up. As they were praying, I started to feel self-conscious, thinking these ladies were praying so fervently but nothing was happening. I felt sorry for them because they were trying so hard. Still, there was no evidence of the gift of tongues. However, it did not seem to faze them one bit. They were definitely tenacious and well-seasoned in intercession, that much I knew for sure.

I don't know how long I sat there. It seemed like an eternity. I finally got my mind off "me" and what "they" were doing and started to worship and praise God. In the next moment, a heavenly language started to flow from my lips. I looked up and I had a vision of Jesus at the top of a huge staircase surrounded by clouds and He was looking down at me with piercing eyes of liquid love. I don't know how long I sat there but suddenly, I jumped up and picked up every one of those ladies and twirled them around. These ladies said they saw a brilliant, radiant glow enveloping my countenance. I never saw it. However, the "radiance" stayed with me for the next three days. Wherever I went, people noticed it and commented. One person, when I walked up to her, fell back unto her chair. I really did not understand all that was happening except that I had never in my life experienced such joy, nor had I ever felt so extremely happy. Everything and everyone appeared to be beautiful.

About a month or so later, these same ladies came up to me in church and asked me if I was using my "prayer language." I said, "No, I thought it was just for that one time." Since I was given this new understanding, I started to use my new prayer language every day. It was not long before the devil began to bombard me with his lies, telling me that I was just making it all up and that it was stupid. Of course, he doesn't like it when God's children pray in an unknown tongue, because every time we do, we step on his head as we are moving in the power and authority of a believer!

And there appeared to them tongues as of fire distributing themselves, and they rested on each one of them. And they were all filled with the Holy Spirit and began to speak with other tongues, as the Spirit was giving them utterance. (Acts 2:3-4)

Chapter 8

Hippies, Drugs, and Massive Mercy

BANG BANG, BANG, went the door. Oh, how I wish the doorbell worked. The noise was so loud, and I did not want my napping children to wake up. I quickly rushed down the stairs to see what all this racket was about.

We lived in this big, beautiful rented house, after arriving in New York from our home state of California. I called it, "Peter Rabbit's house," because we were told the illustrator of Peter Rabbit books used to live there. Every Easter, we received letters addressed to Peter Rabbit. The place filled us with a childlike sense of wonder and awe.

I just knew something great was going to happen to me while living there!

The house was located less than an hour north of Manhattan in Rockland County. Babbling brooks and lush foliage made up this heavenly landscape. The floor to ceiling windows throughout the house gave us a view that was absolutely breathtaking; blue skies and fluffy white clouds, something extremely rare in Southern California in the 1970s due to the high smog pollution.

This was just too wonderful for me. No more smog. No more earthquakes. No more red eyes!

There were three stone fireplaces, two of which were six feet wide and four feet high, sitting on an imported Italian floor that had zone heating so the tile would be warm. That definitely worked for me since my feet were usually cold.

I wasn't sure what was going to happen to me there, but I had a sense that it was going to be very good. Maybe, I would even try my hand at painting, since my father was an artist. Perhaps some of that ability had, in some small way, transferred to me. It wasn't long before I realized that it wasn't my gift.

Oh yes, the banging on my front door. It finally stopped by this time, and I was grateful my napping children did not wake up.

When I opened the door, I found the mailman holding a letter for my husband's brother. What I did not realize at the time was that the envelope had drugs inside.

His brother lived in a small house just in front of the larger one we rented on the same property. Ordinarily, I would have just taken the letter without looking; however, this time, I looked at the name on the front of the envelope and told the mail carrier, "You have the wrong Yusko, please try the front house," and so they left.

"Thank you, thank you, thank you, Lord, for your obvious intervention on our behalf!"

The authorities had our house and my brother-in-law's house, which were located on the same property, under surveillance for many months. They assumed that because we were living in the large, luxurious home in the back, that we were the "Big Kahuna" drug dealers supplying the county. They patiently waited across the street, hidden next to a large building, like lions eagerly seeking their prey. They waited for just the right opportunity, in order to make the necessary arrests.

Shortly thereafter to my astonishment, I looked down from an upstairs window and was horrified at what I saw.

The property was filled with local police, sheriff cars, and FBI agents; everywhere there were law enforcement officers swarming the grounds.

Suddenly, my memory was jarred while I remembered the words of my husband just a few weeks earlier. He said, "Sallie,

Everywhere there were law enforcement officers swarming the grounds.

I don't want you to go inside my brother's house anymore. When you went to borrow a cup of sugar please know that those were not cooking ingredients my brother and his friends were rolling up in tinfoil."

Suddenly, law enforcement agents busted into the small house below, forcing their way in after my sister-in-law received the envelope. They proceeded to search for drugs, all while my five-year-old nephew stood helplessly looking on. Next thing I knew, she was whisked away in a squad car! I'm not sure where my brother-in-law was at the time, but they did arrest him later that day.

My husband's brother and friends were all "hippies" dealing and doing drugs; not so much as to make a monetary profit, as it was to just supply drugs to their friends so everyone would be happy.

His brother had a "Robin Hood" mindset. He considered my husband and I to be "fat cats," only interested in making money. He said he had found God in the trees and considered himself to be quite "spiritual," wanting nothing to do with the establishment.

My brother-in-law was kept from serving a very long jail sentence only by the grace and mercy of a compassionate God, who made a way when there was seemingly no way in the natural. Instead, a miracle was performed.

A technicality kept him from this fate!

We know it was not coincidence, but divine providence. He cried out to the Lord, and the Lord heard and delivered him. How great is His mercy!

Al's brother during his "hippie" days

This poor man cried, and the Lord heard
him and saved him out of all his troubles.

(Psalms 34:6)

Everything I did to try and control my circumstances during this tumultuous time was not working. Everything was falling apart right before my very eyes. I could hardly believe it! I was trying to raise two small children with the chaos of drugs and "hippies" always on the property. My husband was never home, working day and night for an oil additive company, making money. Again, my plans for having this "perfect" little family and lifestyle were crumbling, and I felt helpless to do anything about it.

When I was a child, I determined in my heart that one day, as an adult and in my own house, I would avoid all the insanity. But sometimes, no matter how hard we try, no matter if we cross all of our "t's" and dot all our "i's," and do all the right things... circumstances beyond our control just happen, life sometimes throws you a curveball when you least expect it.

Remember when I said that I felt "something great" was going to happen to me in that house?

Well, I am able to see how God was using the drugs of my brother-in-law, along with other scenarios and situations along the way, that were encroaching upon the lifestyle that

I so desperately wanted to create, to ultimately bring me to the end of myself, and into a relationship with Him. I am forever grateful.

I came to know Jesus Christ as my Lord and Savior at the age of twenty-seven, and my life was forever changed. Many decades later, I am here to say that God has never left me, failed me, or forsaken me. He is good, all the time!

> *"You will seek Me and find Me when you*
> *search for Me with all your heart."*
>
> (Jeremiah 29:13)

My husband, his brother, and our dog Precious,
decades later in Florida

Chapter 9

The Birthing of a Ministry

It was Sunday, June 24th, 1984. We began our first church service in Schenectady, New York. There was a small number in attendance, and during my husband's message, he asked for those who would be interested in knowing the vision of the Lord for New Hope Gospel Fellowship to stay afterward for a meeting in the front pews.

He had approximately ten days to prepare for the first Sunday morning. A sweet lady in the Lord had offered to print up some song sheets. A pastor's daughter from Schoharie County consented, after much pressure from her mom, to play the piano.

We had virtually no idea of what was going to happen, but my husband knew that he had heard from God and that he was in His perfect will.

He put $100 down for purchase of the church building and asked the broker, "Please don't cash the check." We needed $15,000 within ten days or the church building would go back on the market. He shared this with the original fifteen people who waited after the Sunday morning service to hear the vision the Lord had given him. He knew that he had heard from the Lord, and the Lord told him to buy this building. He knew God was in it but did not know how we were going to get the $15,000. He asked the broker for the key to the building, to which the reply came, "No, I want to show the

New Hope Gospel Fellowship,
Schenectady, New York

Left to right: daughter Carrie, me, daughter Kelli and Al,
being prayed for by Pastors Tom Hatcher, Carl Johnson and
the presbytery of New City Gospel Fellowship, New City, NY

building." Al said, "My $100 is taking it off the market, and I need to have the key so I can go into the building each day to pray." So, the broker relinquished the key. I am sure he didn't believe that we could raise $15,000 for the down payment.

On a Monday afternoon, Al received a phone call from two ladies who said they would like to take him out to lunch. They wanted to discuss the $15,000 need. That was great news! These sweet saints believed their husbands would most wholeheartedly help contribute part, if not all, of the money. Needless to say, we were rejoicing and praising God!

Al mentioned to the ladies that he was meeting with an accountant, an attorney, and the former pastor of the church and the presbytery at 6 p.m. this coming Friday, and that they would leave by 7 p.m. because they kept the Sabbath at sundown.

It was Wednesday, and he still had not heard a peep from either of these women. By Thursday, he called one of the ladies and asked her, "How is everything coming along?" The response was, "Oh well, I guess the Lord is going to have to provide for the down payment somehow because at this time, my husband can't do what I thought he could do." That meant no finances for the down payment. The next comment was something to the effect, "But we are going to believe that God will bring in the finances." Then Al said, "Well, how about sister so and so?" She hesitated and then said, "Well, maybe you should speak to her directly."

He did call the other lady, and it was generally the same scenario. It was Thursday, at approximately 1 p.m., and there was no money and Friday was just around the corner. Leaving our house, he went to the church building, walked inside, and envisioned what the Lord had shown him the first time he entered the building. Above the altar was the name "JESUS." He saw in the Spirit what later became a physical reality. He saw people with their hands raised worshipping the Lord, and the sanctuary filled with His presence and the cloud of glory.

He saw in the Spirit thousands coming to the altar for salvation. He saw people being healed and set free. He saw God moving mightily as a cloud. His presence was so rich and thick that he knew he had heard from the Lord as He showed him the same vision overview for the second time.

He spoke out loud to the Lord, "What we don't need is any more abominations or any more people saying, 'Thus, saith the Lord' and it not coming to pass. Lord, if I have missed you for some reason, please remove me from ministry." He felt the peace in his spirit, so he continued to wait and pray.

Just then, a door opened. A woman walked in and said, "The Lord sent me; here is $1000. Who do I make the check out to?" He said, "Make it out to New Hope Gospel Fellowship." The lady said she didn't like that name and pulled the check back towards herself. He said, "That is the name the Lord has given me." Then she handed the check back. Even in the infancy of this ministry, we saw the controlling spirits trying to take over. He thanked the lady for her donation.

TWENTY MINUTES LATER...

A young couple showed up and asked if they could go up front to the altar of the church to pray and seek the Lord as to what He would have them do. Please understand that these people did not call. They were divinely sent to show up just as he was sent that very same day. He saw the young couple talking directly to the altar, not to each other, but to the altar, as if there were three people having a conversation. After the conversation and prayer, they presented him with a $3,500 check made out to him personally because they didn't know the name of the church. Within half an hour, the same scenario happened again.

Another person came, as God had directed, and gave another $1000 check. Shortly thereafter, a lady came with a $2,500 check and said, "Pastor, this is what the Lord told me to give you, a check made out to cash." He looked at the $2,500 check in his hand and then handed it back to her and said, "This is not the amount of money that God told you to bring." She looked at him with astonishment. He could not believe that he actually said that to her. Then he continued, "Take the check and come back with the full amount that the Lord told you to bring." She started to cry and said, "You're right, I did lie; the amount was $5000. That was the amount the Lord told my husband to give because we were putting our tithes in a special account for many months and my husband said to give the full amount, but I was disobedient to God, just as I was disobedient to my husband." She left crying, with the $2,500 check.

After she left, my husband said, "My God, what did I do? Why didn't I hold on to the check and tell her to bring a second with the other half which would have been $2,500?" Within the hour, she came back with a check for $5000.

This type of giving continued until there was $14,500 in his hand on Friday night at 6 p.m. Checks were made out to New Hope Gospel Fellowship, and checks were made out to cash. Checks were made out to Al Yusko, money orders, and blank checks.

Sitting around our dining room table, the presbytery from the denomination that we were purchasing the church from said, "Wow, look at all those checks, you must be some fundraiser." He looked at the individual and was going to share what had happened but felt he wouldn't comprehend this move of God. So, there we sat with $14,500.

Just then, the phone rang. It was a man from the area who heard what the need was. He had not been to the Sunday morning church service. He said, "Pastor Al, I understand you need $15,000 for a down payment to purchase the church building." Al said, "Yes we do." The man said, "How much are you short?" First of all, how did he know we were short, or even about the need? So, I said, "We are $500 short, but we really need $1000 for miscellaneous startup costs like communion trays, offering plates, etc." He then said, "Don't push it. Send someone over to pick up the $500." Al said, "Well, you can't blame us for trying," and they both laughed. My husband sent me to pick up the check. $15,000 was raised supernaturally in a day and a half by the hand of God, the Great Provider, Jehovah Jireh!

Pastors Al and Sallie in sanctuary of New Hope Gospel Fellowship

We call this, "The Birthing of a Ministry" and we give God all the honor and praise for the "Miracle of New Hope."

New Hope Gospel Fellowship went on to thrive, prosper, and become a beacon of hope for the downtrodden, hungry, and hopeless in Schenectady, New York.

The community outreaches, food pantries, soup kitchens, and tent crusades impacted our city with love, the gospel, and the good news of Jesus Christ. God's blessings and favor on the ministry were evident to all.

God raised up a man of Italian and Polish descent who had great faith and a big vision. A man who knew that nothing, absolutely nothing, was impossible with God! When you reach out to the very least of these, you are touching the very heart of God. Jesus made that clear in this excerpt from "The Parable of the Sheep and the Goats."

"'For I was hungry, and you gave Me something to eat; I was thirsty, and you gave Me something to drink; I was a stranger, and you invited Me in; naked, and you clothed Me; I was sick, and you visited Me; I was in prison, and you came to Me.' Then the righteous will answer Him, 'Lord, when did we see You hungry, and feed You, or thirsty, and give You something to drink? And when did we see You a stranger, and invite You in, or naked, and clothe You? When did we see You sick, or in prison, and come to You?' The King will answer and say to them, 'Truly I say to you, to the extent that you did it to one of these brothers of Mine, even the least of them, you did it to Me.'" (Matthew 25:35-40)

Ministering the Word of God

Chapter 10

Angels on Assignment

*A*nticipation and excitement filled the air when suddenly, without warning, hot coffee splashed everywhere. "Oh no," I thought, "Not now!"

As we embarked upon this new adventure, our two young daughters were fast asleep in the backseat of our car and we had barely gone five minutes from our home when my husband was soaked with hot, black coffee. He made a sharp turn on a desolate, winding, country road that had many twists and bends, when suddenly, out flew the coffee from the car's cupholder splashing everywhere.

It was very early on a Sunday morning with not a soul, much less another car, in sight. We were on our way to Lake Winnipesaukee in New Hampshire to attend a Christian retreat/camp for families.

My husband said, "Wait in the car" and got out to look for something in the trunk to help wipe up the mess. The sun was just starting to come up, barely peeking through some of the dense fog that only a few minutes earlier was hovering over the roadway. Our young daughters were then wide awake!

Shortly thereafter, Al came around to the front of the car to tell me what had just transpired over the last few minutes. A look of shock graced his face as he proceeded to tell us, "A very nice man, with a New Hampshire license plate, pulled up behind us to see if he could offer his assistance." My husband thanked him, and said, "We are all okay, just a little wet and messy." He then marveled at what a "coincidence" it was to see a car with a New Hampshire plate on a desolate road so early Sunday morning!

Hmmm...

He told the gentleman that he was on the way to New Hampshire but did not have a map. The stranger immediately pulled from his pocket a map of New Hampshire already marked with a yellow highlighter, starting from the exact spot where we were at that moment to the exact location of the lake and retreat where we were headed.

Hmmm...

Thanking him very much for his help, while still trying to comprehend what had just happened, Al walked back to the drivers' side of our car and began telling us everything that just took place.

We looked at one another in awe and said, "Do you think that was an angel?" When we all looked back, there was no man...no car...not a soul... not a man nor beast in sight... just my husband, standing there with a map of New Hampshire in his hands that perfectly outlined our destination start to finish with a yellow highlighter. We looked at one another in awe and said, "Do you think that was an angel?"

We concluded that we had just had an encounter with an angelic being in human form. We drove away still pondering the magnitude of that moment and thanking the Lord for sending one of His angels to help us. God knows...we needed help!

ANOTHER MIRACLE

"Angels on mountain road cliff...This is it...I am going to be dead!" These thoughts were whirling through my head when my car became airborne!

I had just finished dropping off our youngest daughter, Kelli, at nursery school and was on my way home. The landscape was covered with freshly fallen snow and there were twinkling ice crystals everywhere. Oh, the beauty…the magnificence! It was almost too much for a native California girl like me to take in all at once. Breathtaking would be an understatement.

Suddenly, my car got out of control, and I immediately put on the brakes. Not a good idea! No one told me that when you hit ice, you should never apply your brakes. What did I know? I grew up in sunny Southern California, where my biggest car concerns were no more surfboards flying off the roof of my car.

My basic instinct and frog-like reflexes went into overdrive when the car started to slip and slide. The next thing I knew, it sailed through the air, dangling over the cliff, ready to drop. Oddly enough, I experienced total peace while this was happening.

Immediately, my car was literally picked up and turned totally around and put back on the road again. I was facing the mountainous embankment. Realizing what had just happened, and understanding the law of gravity, fear immediately gripped my heart.

A few minutes later, a police car whizzed right past me while I was sitting in my car numb, trying to get a hold of myself. I was starting to get angry. Couldn't that officer see that my car had skid into the mountainside and that I was a woman in distress? I was just beside myself.

Well, I managed to pull my car around and get it going in the right direction. As I proceeded down the mountain, I saw a school bus that had slid and was in trouble. "Oh Lord," I thought, "so that's why he raced past me, knowing there was a much more serious situation up ahead. No wonder You hate it so much when we prejudge without knowing the whole story!"

I cried as I pulled into our driveway. My husband said I sounded like a dying raccoon when he saw me slowly wobbling out of my car. Of course, who knows if raccoons even cry, much less dying ones, but that's beside the point. I was pretty shaken by then and could hardly get out the words to tell him what had happened. Needless to say, I'm sure he was perplexed, but that's why I would often remind him that the Lord thinks it's a good idea that men live with their wives in an understanding way.

When things settled down, I wanted to go back up that mountain road and show him where my car headed off the cliff. When we arrived, we got out of the car, and you could still see the tire marks in the snow, making us realize that there was no earthly explanation for why my car had not gone over the cliff.

Understanding the full gravity of the situation, a gentle quietness filled the air as we drove back to our home.

> *For he will give His angels charge concerning you, to guard you in all your ways. They will bear you up in their hands, that you do not strike your foot against a stone.*
>
> (Psalms 91:11-12)

The Christmas Miracle

The newly fallen snow softly blanketed the stately Tudor-like building that was the home of New Hope Gospel Fellowship Church, located in Schenectady, New York.

It was a little less than two weeks before Christmas, and everyone was making last minute preparations for the upcoming outreach.

Inside the church, the three pastors, staff, and a host of volunteers were busily wrapping and labeling hundreds of gifts for that evening's annual Christmas giveaway we put on for our community. Each present was marked either for a boy or a girl, with the appropriate age written on the outside. The congregants of New Hope were extremely generous, bringing to church gifts for the less fortunate. Though most of them were not rich by this world's standard, they possessed the "spirit of giving," and it was always done with a cheerful heart.

Christmas music filled the air, playing softly in the background, reminding us all that December 25th was approaching all too quickly. It caused a bit of anxiety, especially for those of us who had a tendency to procrastinate. Yikes!

The news rapidly spread each year about the gift giveaway and about the Christmas dinner at New Hope. The amount of families that came seemed to double each year. After looking at the large crowd gathering outside, waiting for the festivities to begin, our assistant pastor said to my husband, "We do not have enough presents. What are we going to do?"

The outreach was soon to begin, when a truck pulled up outside the church filled with wrapped presents. The man in the truck brought the presents into the church, and the as- **"We do not have enough presents. What are we going to do?"** sociate pastor quickly ran to get my husband so he could come meet this man and inquire where he was from. By the time they got downstairs, the man and his truck were gone!

Families, with their energetic and sometimes boisterous children, were starting to quickly fill up the sanctuary, all of them scrambling to get a seat in the front row where they could clearly see the colorful presents on the altar. The excitement and enthusiasm were beginning to become contagious.

The giving out of presents was done in an orderly fashion. They would come one at a time, as their age and gender were called, and then return to their seats. When the last child came up, we ended up with five extra wrapped presents. The staff asked my husband if he wanted to give the extras out. He said, "No, put them downstairs and we will keep them for the next outreach."

Monday morning came around, our secretary said there was a single mother in the office with her four children and she said that she was sorry that she was unable to get to the outreach but wondered if there were any presents left.

Well, it just so happened that there were five presents left, and they were marked with the exact ages and genders of her children and there was even one for an adult female!

> *"But the very hairs of your head are all numbered. So do not fear; you are more valuable than many sparrows."* (Matthew 10:30)

We believe that the man who came by the church that snowy December evening with his black pickup filled with wrapped and marked Christmas presents, enough for every family, with five left over for that single mother and her children, was without a doubt, an angel sent on assignment to bless the poor and less fortunate among us.

Chapter 11

Mommy, Don't You Think Jesus Heard You the First Time?

"Oh Jesus, help me...Oh Jesus, help me...Oh Jesus, help me," I kept saying over and over again, at which point my four-year-old daughter looked at me with exasperation on her little face and said:

"Mommy, don't you think Jesus heard you the first time?"

I was in my car driving on a beautiful, clear winter day when suddenly, the weather took a sharp turn for the worse. Icy roads, sleet, and falling snow seemed to appear out of nowhere. This simple childlike statement from my daughter jolted me into reality, making me realize just how stupid I was sounding.

I believe a "spirit of fear" entered into me after my cliff experience, so much so that at the first sight of a snowflake I would not drive unless I absolutely had to.

What I did not know at the time was that if you immediately pray against a "spirit of fear" after any trauma, it protects against fear of that situation taking root and causing bondage.

Falling snowflakes...the very thing that was once an object of beauty and wonderment to me, had become a paralyzing form of fear.

I found myself always checking the weather ahead of time. If snow was predicted, I would make up every excuse in the world not to have to go out. I once even contemplated washing my hair and sticking my head out the window to try and catch a cold if I thought it would keep me from having to be on the roads while it was snowing. I know…it's pitiful. It really is. You would probably never do such a thing. But when fear is present and you find it controlling you, it is gripping, and it makes people think and do unreasonable and irrational things. Thankfully, it was short-lived!

FACING YOUR FEARS

The next Sunday at church, our beloved pastor, Tom Hatcher, prayed a very simple prayer over me, and I knew and believed in my heart that God truly had delivered and set me free.

> *"If the Son makes you free, you will be free indeed."* (John 8:36)

I was so completely set free that I would go out in almost any type of weather without fear. One time, when it was snowing pretty heavily, I told my husband I wanted to drive to the mall because it would not be very crowded. God is good. Don't get me wrong, He doesn't want you to be foolish, but He definitely doesn't want you living in fear or being controlled by a spirit of fear.

> *For God hath not given us the spirit of fear; but of power, and of love, and of a sound mind.* (2 Timothy 1:7 KJV)

I have flown all my life, even from an early age, with no fear whatsoever. Then suddenly, I realized this "fear thing" was starting to grip me concerning flying. Good grief!

It finally came to me how this fear entered. We weren't Christians when my husband was taking flying lessons in the early years of our marriage, hoping to become a commercial airline pilot. There was such a back log of military pilots at the time, who had hundreds, if not thousands of flight hours, that it wasn't feasible to continue with the expensive flight lessons. He would share with me, from time to time, some of the inside information not commonly known to the general public on all the mishaps of planes, flying, etc. He wasn't purposefully trying to put fear in me, just like I was not trying to gross him out when I shared all my nursing stories. They were just simply points of interest to us both at the time, a matter of casual conversation in those days.

I have since learned about the power of "death and life" in the tongue.

I have since learned about the power of "death and life" in the tongue. I believe it was during that time, however, when fear got into my spirit, and I allowed it to take root until it grew "over the top."

This I know for certain; I would encourage you to never allow yourself to listen to anything that could cause you to become fearful. If airplanes are your issue, don't read about all the airplane crashes and mishaps. Turn off the TV, put down the newspapers, and excuse yourself from the room if it's being discussed.

> *Finally, brethren, whatever is true, whatever is honorable, whatever is right, whatever is pure, whatever is lovely, whatever is of good repute, if there is any excellence and if anything worthy of praise, dwell on these things.* (Philippians 4:8)

The fear would be so gripping that my hands would literally drip with perspiration, my heart would race, and I'd squeeze my husband's hand so tight while flying that I'm surprised I did not cut off his circulation. The whole time I would be praying—praying in English, praying in the Spirit, and trying to remember scriptures to quote. I could not even read or eat while flying.

I would try to remind myself just how ridiculous this was for a believing Christian. "After all," I reasoned, "a 'spiritual' Christian would consider this a great time to share the gospel."

Well, that was not me! I didn't even want anybody to know I was a Christian when I flew for obvious reasons. I just wanted to get on the ground as quickly as possible. I mean, it was embarrassing!

I don't know exactly when it happened. I just know that one day, while about 30,000 feet in the air looking out at the clouds, the Lord started to gently and clearly speak to me. I must have been settled enough in my spirit to be able to hear His voice.

He reminded me of how very much I loved my children and how I would always protect them and do anything for them. He reminded me that if I could love and care for my children that much, how much more could He love and care for me, in whatever situation I found myself.

> *There is no fear in love; but perfect love casts out fear.* (1 John 4:18)

That simple, loving illustration from the Holy Spirit was just what it took to break the yoke of bondage off me. I felt a strong sense that whether the plane I was on at that time, or any other plane for that matter, flies or crashes, that He is always with me. It would be His peace, just like I experienced in the midst of my cliff experience. It would be His peace that would surround me. He would be right there holding me, and in His Presence all fear must flee, making room for the fullness of joy and the peace that passes all understanding.

> *"Have I not commanded you? Be strong and courageous! Do not tremble or be dismayed, for the Lord your God is with you wherever you go."* (Joshua 1:9)

"Peace I leave with you; My peace I give to
you; not as the world gives do I give to you.
Do not let not your heart be troubled, nor let
it be fearful."   (John 14:27)

God quieted my soul, and once again, brought deliverance right there at 30,000 feet.

CHARLES MANSON AND THE FEAR OF STAYING ALONE

The infamous Charles Manson and LaBianca murders took place not far from where we lived, and the culprits had not yet been caught.

We were living in Southern California and everyone living in that general vicinity was living on pins and needles. It was during this time that I became very afraid to stay in my home alone.

When we left California for New York in the early 70s, we were living in the big house that I mentioned earlier, where the law enforcement thought we were drug dealers. The house was very isolated and set back from the road without much lighting. One evening, while reading the Scriptures, I came to Psalms 4:8.

In peace I will both lie down and sleep, •
for You alone, O Lord, make me to dwell in
safety.   (Psalms 4:8)

I read it, immediately believed it, and was never again afraid to stay alone. The Lord brought instant deliverance, simply by believing His Word with all my heart.

Shortly thereafter, the same house was broken into while we were out, we believe by "druggies." We found out later that it was some of my brother-in-law's acquaintances who were looking for money.

But there wasn't any...

Only a glass jar filled with pennies that was left on the bed, probably in disgust that they were unable to find more. There was nothing in the house of any real value to take. We left mostly everything we owned in California, thinking we would return someday, or at least that's what I secretly thought. As Proverbs 16:9 reveals, many are the plans in the mind of a man, but the Lord directs his steps.

The fear of staying alone had completely lost its grip on me. The Lord's peace prevailed even in the aftermath of having our home violated. We knew that it was the Lord, and only the Lord Himself, who made us to dwell in safety.

Chapter 12

Divine Appointments at 30,000 Feet

*N*ever underestimate the power of a cookie…especially a chocolate chip cookie.

It was in the month of November, more specifically the week before Thanksgiving, when our oldest daughter, Carrie, decided to take a plane ride to San Francisco to see her grandmother for the holidays. I was hoping she would stay with us and the rest of our family living in New York, but that was purely selfish on my part. I knew in my heart that her grandmother would be so happy to see her.

Our daughter had been a single mom for over four years, and I had prayed so many prayers, for so many years, that I was sure that I must have worn the Lord out with my constant petitions. It was during that time that I felt she had drifted away from the things of God from whence she'd come. There always seemed to be a strong pull of this world's fleeting pleasures beckoning.

Never underestimate the power of a cookie especially a chocolate chip cookie.

I refused to give up as I continued asking, seeking, and knocking for a godly husband for her. The red carpet in our den had become threadbare where I kneeled each day and night to pray, oftentimes with tears streaming down my face for my precious child.

On one such occasion, I again found myself weeping before the Lord. I felt like He was telling me to go to the book of Jeremiah and read chapter 31, verse 16.

> *Thus says the Lord, "Restrain your voice from weeping and your eyes from tears; for your work will be rewarded, declares the Lord, and they will return from the land of the enemy. There is a hope for your future, declares the Lord, and your children will return to their own territory."* (Jeremiah 31:16-17)

Instantly, peace came...

I knew immediately that God was speaking directly to me concerning a mother's heartache and that He indeed had heard my prayers. This brought great comfort to my soul. I was filled to overflowing with His peace; that wonderful, glorious peace that once again passes all understanding and human reasonings.

Let the reader please understand that whether you are a mother or a father, either physically or spiritually, the Lord God is no respecter of persons and what He has done for me, He will do for you and your children. His Word never returns void but always accomplishes that which it is sent out to do.

The time had come when we found ourselves standing in the Albany International Airport giving my daughter and our five-year-old grandson hugs, kisses, and homemade chocolate chip cookies for their journey. We know, at least in our family, that all trips seem to be better (in fact, everything seems to be better) when you have chocolate chip cookies.

My husband and I stood there, waving goodbye as they left to board their plane. We missed them already.

Little did we realize that this was a "set-up" from heaven, a divine appointment, if you will. Once again, Kevin Zadai says, "It's all rigged."

My daughter had a seat on the plane next to a young man who lived about thirty minutes away from us at the time. During the plane ride, my five-year-old grandson went to sleep for the entire trip to California. This was really unheard of for this very active little boy!

After their meal onboard the flight (they fed you more than peanuts in those days), my daughter offered the young man some chocolate chip cookies, which made a very "mouth-watering" impression on him I was later told. She of course, not having a "shy" nature, asked him if he wanted his sausage, to which he replied, "No, you can have it," and she promptly removed it from his plate with her fork.

This was only the beginning…

During that five-hour flight, the young man and my daughter struck up various conversations that lasted the entire trip until they arrived at their destination…good ol' San Francisco, where Tony Bennett left his heart.

The Lord miraculously continued to weave together a beautiful tapestry of divine circumstances.

They both stayed in San Francisco for five days and ended up flying back to Albany on the same day, on the same plane, seated next to each other. As if that were not enough, our grandson fell asleep for the duration of that flight as well, allowing the two of them to continue where they left off just a few short days earlier. One of the things they found out was that Patrick (the young man that I have been talking about) was an engineer working for General Electric and he was looking to buy a house.

What a coincidence! Our daughter just happened to sell real estate. Coming straight from the airport to our home, she briskly walked through the door holding the sourdough bread we had asked her to bring from Fisherman's Wharf. I knew instantly something had happened to her. She had a "different" look. Yes, it was a different look! A look that only a mother could know. She said, "Mom, I only brought you one loaf of bread this time because I gave the other one away to a man that I met on the airplane." I replied, "What? You are seriously kidding, right? I mean, I love, love, love, love that sourdough bread from San Francisco. What were you thinking?"

Patrick on his wedding day, with my young grandson, Timothy

I told her that the man she had been dating off and on for over a year was in our den waiting to see her. We both realized she needed to go in and at least say "hello" and acknowledge his presence.

Later that day, she told me all about her encounter with the young engineer from Clifton Park and the chocolate chip cookies. She told me all the things they talked about and how our precious grandson, Timmy, blissfully slept on both of the flights.

In the ensuing months, she sold Patrick a house and then moved into it. He moved back to his parents' house for the time being.

A little more than nine months later…they were married!

Our grandson, Timmy, shouted for all to hear in a very LOUD voice, "Yes!" as they were being pronounced husband and wife. The church was filled with laughter and tears. It was glorious and amazing, so much more than I could have ever imagined.

I would have despaired unless I had believed
that I would see the goodness of the Lord in
the land of the living. (Psalms 27:13)

I am telling you this story to encourage you to never give up, NEVER! Who knows if you might get the impression to take a plane ride somewhere, or go someplace you have never been before, or do something that you've never done before? Don't limit God. He is a big God who loves to give good gifts to his children and do exceedingly and abundantly above and beyond all that we could ever think or ask.

Sometimes it feels like it takes a thousand years for some of the answers to prayer to manifest...

"At the same time, I have come to know over these many years, that You God are always faithful and that Your ways are much higher than my ways or man's ways.

"Lord, help us to remember that Your timing is always perfect! You are never late or early. Surely, you direct our paths when we trust in You with all our hearts, and we don't lean on our own understanding, and when we acknowledge You in all our ways.

"Thank You God for answered prayers...and oh yes, thank you for those chocolate chip cookies!"

Patrick, son-in-love, and daughter, Carrie

Al and Sallie, with their dog Precious, in Florida 2008

Chapter 13

No Carbon Copies

$\mathcal{W}$ho are you? Stop trying to be a man-pleaser and instead please God! You are one of a kind. Be who you were created to be! This is a philosophy of life that we all need to live by.

Make no mistake, aggression and passivity can wreak havoc on relationships.

Many of us have had to face dysfunction at one time or another in ourselves and others. Bishop Mark J. Chironna states, *"From a spiritual perspective, there is no one who is not dysfunctional."*[2]

Passive and aggressive behaviors, and the beliefs associated with these behaviors, are learned very early in one's life. These patterns can continue throughout each of the succeeding generations, and if not recognized, dealt with, or worse than that, simply denied, can usher in self-defeating behaviors for future generations.

I passively withdrew from the battle again and again, avoiding conflict at any cost, even at the cost of not expressing my own identity and not becoming the person that God really created me to be in the first place. My husband had learned some of his mother's controlling behaviors, and I had learned some of my mother's passive behaviors, which were hindering us both from becoming or receiving the very best that God had for us.

In the perfect timing of the Holy Spirit, our Teacher began to lovingly show us where we both needed to be set free from these unhealthy behaviors. When the Lord first started to give me revelation on this matter, I started to obey and implement what He was teaching me. Well, it did not fly so well with my husband at first. Recognizing that the dynamic of our relationship was changing from what had been so familiar, he would say to me, "Where is that sweet, little nineteen-year-old I married?" I would reply, "She is dead and never coming back!"

When it was all said and done, God faithfully revealed to us those areas in our relationship that needed to change. We both allowed the correction of the Holy Spirit because we really knew deep down in our hearts that it would all work for good. We survived the adjusting process, along with the ups and downs and bumps along the road, and you will too! As a result, our marriage and our love and respect for one another grew even stronger.

Passive people hurt themselves first, so as not to risk hurting others.

We shared a greater freedom in intimate communication, becoming all that God originally created us to be.

> *And we know that God causes all things to work together for good to those who love God, to those who are called according to His purpose.* (Romans 8:28)

Passive people hurt themselves first, so as not to risk hurting others. The passive personality (likened to Ahab of the Bible) is often attracted to the aggressive and controlling personality (likened to Jezebel of the Bible).

Jesus lived ASSERTIVELY. He spoke the truth for in denying truth, He would be denying Himself.

> *"I am the way, and the TRUTH, and the life."* (John 14:6)

Jesus gives all people the freedom of choice without trying to control them. Speaking assertively, He always went to the "heart" of the matter, which at times left his enemies enraged and gnashing their teeth.

He certainly was not passive or fearful when dealing with the religious leaders of his day. He just called it "like it was."

> *"So you, too, outwardly appear righteous to men, but inwardly you are full of hypocrisy and lawlessness."* (Matthew 23:28)

Operating in the boldness of a lion and still the gentleness of a dove, calling "a spade a spade" will inevitably turn out for the good, no matter what situation you may find yourself. Never shrink back when you know the Holy Spirit is prompting you to speak something you would rather not speak. Dietrich Bonhoeffer, the well-known, German theologian who resisted Hitler, explains, *"Obedience is better than doubt and reflection."*

Sometimes people in ministry can confuse subservience with submissiveness and give improper counsel. Submissive behavior is being supportive, agreeable, and willing. Subservient behavior is passively giving up one's rights. For example: If a husband asks his wife to sin against God, should she be submissive and agree? Of course not!

"Obedience is better than doubt and reflection."

Never operate in the "spirit of fear" regarding any real or imagined possible repercussions from speaking up. Realize that you are ultimately helping others by giving them a chance to make a choice–either embracing or refusing truth. Then, leave it in God's hands.

"Rest, release, relax, and receive" are the very words I have heard over and over again from the Holy Spirit for my own life. It is a process...trust me!

How will you know for sure if it's the Holy Spirit telling you to speak? You will know because it won't be vindictive or mixed with hatred, guile, or bitterness. Always check and re-check your heart motives. That is a good start. If we ask and expect to receive wisdom from God, He promises to generously give it to us, if we ask in faith and not doubt.

> *But if any of you lacks wisdom, let him ask*
> *of God, who gives to all generously and with-*
> *out reproach, and it will be given to him.*
>   (James 1:5)

> *Behold, You desire truth in the innermost*
> *being, And in the hidden part You will make*
> *me know wisdom.*   (Psalms 51:6)

It is wise to remember that there is a time for everything as the book of Ecclesiastes tells us that there is:

> *A time to be silent and a time to speak.*
>   (Ecclesiastes 3:7)

I cannot stress enough the importance of God's timing in a matter. If you miss it and it was not the "right" timing, don't beat yourself up. We've all have missed it, if we are honest with ourselves. His mercies are new every morning. Get rid of "if only." If only I had said this, instead of that…if only I had… yada, yada, yada. Instead, just say, "Next time, I will…"

A wise man will always weigh his words and think before he speaks. If one just blurts out hurtful words, it leaves the other individual feeling like he or she has just been vomited on. I assure you, that is probably not God.

The Holy Spirit, who is called a Helper in the Bible, will teach you how to be assertive while at the same time walking in love. He will also fill you with the confidence that comes from being in Christ.

The devil is a liar from the beginning. Truth will always bring freedom.

Shame, guilt, and various fears are all entwined in a complicated root system that contributes to passive behavior. As someone who once walked in passivity, oftentimes I would not speak up for myself, and tended to think much less of myself than others, until the truth of God's word set me free.

Aggressive people, on the other hand, use control and manipulation to get their opinions made known. They are good at intimidation, which makes it easy to "shut down" the passive personality.

Passive and aggressive personalities are equally destructive. Giving your God-given authority and power to another is just as damaging as it is to take that same God-given authority away from your fellow man. It is possible to operate in each of these two dimensions at various times, with one of the behaviors being the more dominate and noticeable part of a personality.

Passive people choose to live the "lie" and end up paying the price for not confronting the aggressive people in their lives.

This was true for me for a good part of my life. I like to call it "living in la la land." I'd often pretend that everything was "perfect," and try to create this flawless little world, while believing God should be doing something about all these difficult people and situations in my life. In reality, He was patiently waiting for me. He was not in the least bit worried, even with my many prayers, pleading for Him to do something! I believe it was the great evangelist, John Wesley, who said, *"Beware of asking God to do what He is expecting you to do yourself."*

"Beware of asking God to do what He is expecting you to do yourself."

When I started working as an RN in the early 1970s, I was convinced that I got the most difficult people on the planet. Some of the comments of my fellow private duty nurses were as follows: "I will never work for that patient again." After one day, they quit! But oh no, not me! I dutifully stayed way too long in this state of passivity, allowing these "controlling spirits" (patients) to run right over me. Serving in this dysfunction helps no one, certainly not those operating in control or the ones choosing to stay passive. Both behaviors are damaging.

When I made the decision to stand up assertively with the love and truth of Christ, it not only brought spiritual and physical health to my body, it changed many of my relationships as well.

Ruth (in the Bible) did not go back to what was familiar. She stepped out in faith and walked into the unknown. Her courage brought her to her divine destiny. My prayer for you, the reader, is that you will always have the courage to walk in the truth, holding your head up high, knowing that God is for you and not against you.

> *What then shall we say to these things? If*
> *God is for us, who is against us?*
>
> (Romans 8:31)

My mother-in-law, Stella, was so overpowering and controlling that in the early years of my marriage, when she would fly in to visit us, my hands would crack and bleed from the stress. As soon as she left, my hands would clear up. Before she died, she told me that I was the daughter she never had. I would give her baths, manicures, wash and set her hair, take her shopping, and take her to lunch. I sensed she had a new respect for me that was not there in previous years when I would quietly back down to her verbal abuse. I ultimately had to take the responsibility for what I had allowed. This is not about blaming other people in your life. It's about taking personal responsibility for what you allow. When you are "sick and tired of being sick and tired," the teacher will show up when you, the student, are ready. This revelation will set the others free as well, so they can be the very person that God created them to be in the first place.

Several years before Stella died, I was able to lead her to Christ. She said, "But I'm still a Catholic," and I said, "Yes,

Stella, you are still a Catholic and that is wonderful. Jesus does not really care what denomination you are." This is not about a particular church. It's about accepting Christ as your Lord and Savior and turning your life over to the One who gave His life for you.

My own precious mother, who always thought things would get better if only she just moved or remarried, never learned to confront the issues that came her way. She chose instead to remain detached to the difficult and painful circumstances surrounding her life, while numbing her senses with alcohol.

Because these passive (Ahab) and controlling (Jezebel) behaviors are "learned" from early on, the good news is that they can also be "unlearned!" We are NOT victims. As believers, we have all power and authority over the enemy.

> *"Behold, I have given you authority to tread on serpents and scorpions, and over ALL the power of the enemy, and nothing will injure you."* (Luke 10:19)

Listening to or telling yourself the truth might hurt at first. It may even be vehemently denied or rejected. But in the end, for all those who choose to walk in it, it will bring forth the glorious fruit of righteousness, peace, and joy.

I would invite you to take an honest look at some of the patterns of your life, and some of your "learned" responses that may, or may not, have been godly. Check to see where these behaviors might possibly have been skewed. If you find that what you have been doing really isn't working the way you hoped it would, make a U-turn. That's what repentance really is. Simply turn away from what you've been doing, change your thinking, and renew your mind daily in the Word of God. You will begin to see your life dramatically start to change for the better. I will warn you, however, that this might be painful at first, but in the end, it will bring great rewards and pay huge dividends beyond measure. When Jesus left this earth, He did not leave us as orphans. He left the Holy Spirit to help us and guide us daily. He is here to lead us into all truth. As C.S. Lewis wisely pointed out:

> *"You can't go back and change the beginning, but you can start where you are and change the ending."*[3]

I have wonderful news for you. When the "fog" lifts and the Novocain wears off, you will begin to see the light of day and things will change. You are God's masterpiece, one of a kind, not a carbon copy.

Chapter 14

God Wants You Well

It was just another routine day in my life in New City, New York, only this day was exceptionally beautiful. The bright colors of fall were at their peak, splashing the landscape like beautiful waves, as far as the eye could see. I always love it when God displays his wonders.

I was driving our youngest daughter to the pediatrician for her annual checkup. Upon arrival, her doctor did not express anything out of the ordinary during the exam, and I didn't expect him to either.

When he finished the exam, his normally "mask-like" expression had changed to one of concern. He said, "Your daughter has scoliosis, and we must do further testing to determine the extent of the spine curvature." We were then sent to a specialist in New York City, where we were told she had triple curvature of the spine. This was the beginning of a very long journey of tears, tests, and trials.

"Mommy, Mommy" came the familiar sobs of my youngest daughter. "Why is this happening to me? My clothes are all getting holes and tearing in the front and back, from screws in the brace; girls are looking over the top of the girl's bathroom at school just to look at my back brace. Why Mommy, why? I love God. Why is this happening?" These words were blurted out through a floodgate of tears. Any mother knows that when your children are hurting, your heart is absolutely breaking.

I did not know "why." But what I did know was that God knows the beginning to the end. He has seen "the whole movie" so to speak and His ways are not our ways. His ways are perfect, and His plans for us are always good.

> *"For I know the plans that I have for you,*
> *declares the Lord, plans for welfare and not*
> *for calamity to give you a future and a hope."*
> (Jeremiah 29:11)

The orthopedic specialist wanted her to be put in a back brace that had to be worn twenty-three out of twenty-four hours! We told the specialist in New York City that we were going to try other treatments before committing to the suggested treatment.

His ways are perfect, and plans for us are always good.

He did warn us that if her condition worsened, surgery would be required, which would put her in a body cast for many, many months. We thanked him and told him of our great faith in God and His miracle working power. He was very gracious. We left his office and made an appointment to come back in six months.

We proceeded with a chiropractic approach and swimming on almost a daily basis. This type of treatment has been shown to be successful in some cases.

Traumatic would be the best description of our next visit to the doctor's office. As the new x-rays were put on the screen, the doctor said, "I am so sorry to have to tell you this, but your daughter has gotten much worse since your last visit."

Peace flooded my soul at that moment, and not only mine, but my husband's as well. "That's an unthinkable reaction," you might say. How can it be explained? Well, it cannot. It is not natural. It is supernatural!

> *And the peace of God, which surpasses all*
> *comprehension, will guard your hearts and*
> *your minds in Christ Jesus.* (Philippians 4:7)

Here we were receiving horrible news, and yet our hearts were saturated with the peace of God that surpasses all human wisdom and beyond any understanding. Our daughter, however, was crying, crying on the long ride home, crying until finally falling asleep for the night. We felt so helpless, even though we had prayed with her and tried to bring comfort. "Why Mommy and Daddy, why?" There are no words to describe how we felt inside.

The next day, my husband was off on a week-long business trip, and I felt so alone, knowing that only God Himself would be able to get me through this next week.

I knew in my heart "by faith" that the Lord was near, for Scripture tells us that "He is very near the brokenhearted." In His faithfulness, the Lord was helping me to help my child come to understand that even though it does not "look" good, God is good! We must always trust Him, no matter what we see with the natural eye.

It did not make life any easier for our family, especially

our daughter, when she would come home after school telling us about the mean-spirited and nasty comments of some children who would incessantly tease her about her back brace.

Al with our youngest daughter, Kelli

Oral Roberts was coming to New York on a Sunday afternoon, so our family hopped in the car and off we went, driving down the Palisades Parkway to New York City. When we finally arrived and settled in the auditorium, the service had already started and we heard these excited words from our daughter, "I saw my spine in a vision with Jesus' hands right next to my spine praying. Jesus has healed me, I know it!"

Early the next morning, she came bounding into the kitchen, as was often her style, and proceeded to tell me to call the doctor and make an appointment for a confirmation. That's what happens when you raise your kids in the Lord.

When this same child got older, she bought me a book titled, *How to Raise a Teenager*. I hate to admit it, but she was right. I did not know the first thing about raising a teenager!

MONTHS LATER...

Abruptly, a hand shot up one day in Sunday school when the teacher asked the question, "Has anyone ever felt like God didn't love you?" "Yes!"...came the resounding reply. "I felt that way once," my daughter proceeded to tell her story from a child's perspective. The teacher told me afterwards that she practically taught the entire class that morning.

She told the other children that God always loves them, and that He is a good God, even if they were having troubles. She said that one day "Jesus was going to make her spine straight," because she saw Jesus' hands praying next to her spine in a vision. I was later told that Kelli's teacher was crying at that point, while all the children sat "quiet as a mouse" intently listening. However, I never did understand how a mouse could be so quiet, especially if you own a cat in the country. Our cat used to bat mice around for hours. What we heard in the middle of the night was "squeak, squeak, and squeak!" Oh, I thought it was just awful!

The next year, we moved to Schenectady, New York, and entered full time ministry as pastors. During this time, a pastor's wife that I had just met came to our home to pray. The children were at school and my husband was in his office at the church.

As we were praying, she came against the "spirit of infirmity." We bound up that spirit and commanded it to loose its hold in Jesus' name. We broke off the generational curses from the family line. Instantly, the *rhema* word of God entered my heart and I KNEW, I did not presume or just wish, but I KNEW without a shadow

> **What I know is this, God healed our daughter.**

of doubt that indeed, at that very moment, our daughter had been healed. That might mess with some people's theology, but this is not about a theological debate. What I know is this, God healed our daughter.

> *And, behold, there was a woman which had a spirit of infirmity eighteen years, and was bowed together, and could in no wise lift up herself. And when Jesus saw her, he called her to him, and said unto her, "Woman, thou art loosed from thine infirmity."*
>
> (Luke 13:11-12 KJV)

Luke's account goes on to say that this woman was a daughter of Abraham, whom Satan bound for eighteen years. Yes, a daughter of Abraham, a Christian, if you will. Jesus prayed and she immediately straightened up and was healed.

He always made the "religious people" furious because it was done on the Sabbath and not done in accordance to their "expectations" or "methods."

Jesus Christ came that He might destroy the works of the devil and give us an abundant life. The devil, on the other hand, hates you! He wants to steal, kill, and destroy your life.

> *"My people are destroyed for lack of knowledge."* (Hosea 4:6)

Let's not become so stubborn or self-righteous that we miss the covenant blessings of the Lord or get "stuck" in a "religious mindset." It was the religious people who convinced the Romans to nail Jesus to the cross.

*Do not be excessively righteous and do
not be overly wise. Why should you ruin
yourself?* (Ecclesiastes 7:16)

When Jesus spit in the ground and made clay of the spittle and then applied it to the blind man's eyes on the Sabbath, it made the "religious people" furious. That did not mesh with their theology. It was not supposed to be like that. His irreligious methods were not acceptable to their self-righteous mindset. When questioning the blind man about who Jesus was and where He came from, the blind man said, "All I know is that once I was blind but now I see." (See John 9:25) Funny, a miracle took place and then an interrogation followed. God help us.

As some time had passed by then, Kelli's back brace was getting too small and she needed to go yet again for another fitting. Our appointment with the specialist was not for a month. We never did go for the fitting, and the brace sat in the closet without being worn. The night before the appointment, I heard in my spirit the devil laughing. I heard him saying, "She is not healed. You just think she is healed, and she is not!" The devil proceeded to whisper in my ear, thoughts that the pastor's wife who prayed with me was weird. "Spirit of infirmity, phooey! Generational whatever, ridiculous! That doctor is going to give you the opposite of heaven for being so negligent by keeping your child out of her brace for over a month! And you call yourself an RN? Why you ought to be ashamed of yourself!"

These thoughts bombarded me as I unexpectedly caught a glimpse of my daughter's back when she was returning to her bedroom after showering. It was at that exact moment that I saw a huge hump on her back.

I once again heard in my spirit, this very evil, mocking laugh.

I kept all of this to myself while casting down imaginations and rebuking the devil. The next morning, we set out for our three-hour drive to Manhattan. We sang songs and worshipped the Lord all the way to New York City.

THE WAIT THAT SEEMED LIKE AN ETERNITY...

Kelli was the last patient to be seen that day. While x-rays were slowly being put up on the wall, we both held our breath. Our doctor had a resident in the office with him, and after looking at the pictures, a tear started to trickle down his cheek. Then he said: "This is a MIRACLE!"

"This does not just happen instantaneously with triple curvature of the spine. Sometimes as doctors, we find that there are things which simply cannot be explained medically." He proceeded to tell the young doctor with him of our family's faith. When I told him that she had not been in the brace for over a month, it was even a greater confirmation that this truly was divine intervention. He told us that we would no longer need his services but asked if we would please keep in touch because he liked our family very much. And so, we did.

The P.S. on this story...

A little girl came up with her mother to the altar one Sunday morning asking for prayer. The girl had just been diagnosed with scoliosis, and her doctors wanted to put her in a back brace. Kelli asked if she could pray. While praying, she told us that her hands got "hot, like fire"! The church service ended and the next day the girl was taken to her doctor. They returned with a praise report the following Sunday. No evidence of scoliosis! This little girl would not need a back brace or possible surgery. Truly, we all were rejoicing that day!

Why didn't God heal our daughter right away like he did this little girl?

I don't know.

Why do some healings take place instantly?

I don't know.

What I do know is that God hears and answers prayer… albeit it is not always in our "timetable."

I will never stop praying or believing for anyone or anything at any time, just because the outcome was not the way I expected it or because I might not "see" everything turn out the way I think it should at that particular moment.

HEALINGS I HAVE RECEIVED

"There is someone here with a cyst on her ovary, the size of a small lemon, that God wants to heal…would that person raise her hand and come forward."

This was my first encounter with what I thought at the time to be a very bold statement uttered by British evangelist, Eddie Smith. I was a new Christian at the time, and I remember thinking how amazing this all was, that God was so personal, and that He showed how much He cared by telling this evangelist I had a cyst on my ovary, and He wanted to heal it! "How wonderful," I thought. I could scarcely take it in.

The following week, just before the scheduled surgery, the doctor said, "The cyst is gone." Doing several more tests, he was unable to find anything whatsoever on my ovary. I told him how I was prayed for and that God had healed me. I never did get the surgery. Gone is gone!

A minister on television said there was someone who was getting their knees healed, and I knew that was a word for me and I was going to receive it. I am a tennis player, and my knees had to be wrapped in knee braces before I played, because of the pain while bending or walking. I did not care how silly it may have looked. I simply put my hand on the TV and believed God! The next morning, I played tennis without the braces, and my knees have been perfectly fine to date, twenty years later.

One prayer of deliverance has kept me pain-free for over ten years.

I suffered with migraine headaches for more years than I would like to remember. One prayer of deliverance has kept me pain-free for over ten years.

I discovered a lump on my neck two days before going to a healing crusade led by a world-renowned evangelist. I was planning on going to this crusade weeks before this discovery, but God already knew ahead of time just what I would need, and what He would do for me, His child, that day. God is no respecter of persons. What He has done for me, He will most assuredly do for you, too. Believe Him and know that all things are possible with God!

Admittedly, I was very disappointed when the healing evangelist said, "Turn around and pray for the person behind you." He said he had not done this before and emphasized that it was the Lord who was the Healer. I must confess, I was even more disappointed when I turned around and suddenly realized the person behind me could barely speak English. I was not very convinced she even understood my prayer request.

Kelli, as a healthy vibrant adult, and mother of three

I am ashamed to admit it, because I know better, but in my heart, I really did want that well-known healing evangelist to pray for me. However, immediately after the lady with the broken English laid her hands on my neck and prayed, the lump just disappeared. Imagine that!

I am sure the Lord taught a lot of people in that meeting not to yield to the temptation of looking at "the vessel" or "the man or woman of the hour," no matter how anointed they may seem. But instead, to look to God who can use whoever, or whatever He chooses, even a donkey, to accomplish His purposes.

I went home feeling very humbled and happy, meditating on the goodness and greatness of our God.

> *Every good thing given and every perfect gift*
> *is from above, coming down from the Father*
> *of lights, with whom there is no variation or*
> *shifting shadow.* (James 1:17)

Chapter 15

Extravagant Grace

I woke up on a sunny Saturday morning to the sound of a glorious chorus of singing birds just outside my bedroom window. The day was April 1st, 2017. I knew this was going to be a great day!

I was so excited because it was my last day at my private duty job for several weeks. Our family from Michigan was flying to Florida to spend Easter vacation with us.

There was something a little different about this particular morning. I had several gold flakes on my face when I got out of the shower. It seemed different that day, but not necessarily unusual for me. For about the previous ten years, every now and then, I saw a brightly colored gold flake glowing on my face. Years ago, when it was first brought to my attention by others, I tried removing it with a toothpick so I could save it, but it always fell off the toothpick and was gone.

You might be saying, "What? Flakes of gold? That sounds 'flaky' to me, ha-ha." Don't ask me to explain it, because I can't.

But this morning, I had several of them. I was thinking to myself, "Why was I getting so many "kisses" today?" I used to call them "kisses" from God, for lack of a better term. I never talked about it, because most people would just pass it off as weird or think it was probably makeup or something. I might have thought that as well if it didn't happen to me.

I did tell my husband when it first started happening, and he had this strange look on his face without saying anything. "Hmmm," I thought. I guess he was just using wisdom, which of course is always a good idea.

One day, while just stepping out of the shower and wrapping my shivering body in a towel, my husband said, "What is that on your face that is so bright?" I felt somewhat vindicated and happy that he was able to finally see firsthand what I had been seeing all along at various times.

The gold flakes did not seem to come for any particular reason. It's not that I had been necessarily fasting or in deep meditation or even feeling particularly "spiritual" when they appeared. They just seemed to come randomly. Later, I realized that the Lord already knew what was ahead of me that day, and this was just one of His many ways to reveal that He was, and always will be, closer to me than my own breath, and that He would never leave me, fail me, or forsake me.

> *The Lord is the one who goes ahead of*
> *you; He will be with you. He will not fail or*
> *forsake you. Do not fear or be dismayed.*
> (Deuteronomy 31:8)

I was running a bit late for work, so I called out to my husband, who was in the bathroom, and told him I would see him that evening. He knew I tended to get overwhelmed about everything that had to be done. He said, "Don't worry, I will help you to get everything ready for the kids, and we can go grocery shopping on Monday." And off I went.

The night before, my husband suggested that I play an April Fool's joke on my patient, who was always "putting one over" on me almost every time I was in his home. When he was successful, he would laugh and laugh so hard. So, my husband suggested when I went to work in the morning that I tell him I accidently ran into his car. I said, "I don't know if I can really say that," but when I got to work in the morning, my patient had taken a turn for the worse and was not feeling well. Needless to say, it was not the right timing. He was almost ninety years old and he loved to joke around with all the nurses. I liked him so much, as he was witty and sharp as a tack.

At 9 p.m. that night, I said goodbye to my patient and his wife, and told them that I would see them again after Easter. I did not know at the time that I would never go back to work for them.

Finally, home! 9:45 p.m.

My husband always waited up for me before retiring. I opened the door, and there was our Maltese named Precious waiting for me, which was her normal routine. What wasn't normal is that she just sat there at the door and stared at me. I said, "What's wrong Precious? What's wrong? Aren't you happy to see me?" For the past fifteen years, every time I would open the door, she would turn around in circles, jumping up and down beyond excited. Even if I was only gone for fifteen minutes, she would get so excited that you would have thought I had been gone for a year. I am convinced that no one on earth can greet you better than your dog. For a fleeting moment, I thought it was a bit strange that she just sat there staring at me but did not pay too much attention because I was more tired than normal that evening. It had been a very long, twelve-hour shift.

Walking into our family room, I saw the back of my husband's head. He was sitting on the sofa. I called out to him, "Honey, I'm home!" Every night, my husband would lie down on the couch to watch a few programs on television. I never saw him sitting up on the couch. But that night, it was different. Walking closer, I was able to see that his left arm rested on the armrest, with his head slightly tilted upward. He had a very peaceful look on his face. Looking straight at him for the third time, I yelled, "Albert!" No answer. By this time, I think I was in shock, and I was screaming his name over and over and over again. "No! No! This cannot be happening!"

He never woke up.

He did not look dead. From the peace radiating from his face, I knew without a shadow of a doubt that God took him in a nanosecond without any pain. He was not clutching his chest or slumped over. I believe he saw the face of Jesus and the angels coming to take him to his eternal home. My husband always said, when he would hear of others going in a similar manner, that he wanted to enter heaven like that when his time came.

> From the peace radiating from his face, I knew without a shadow of a doubt that God took him in a nanosecond without any pain.

It was 10 p.m. I was dazed and blurry eyed, dressed in my scrubs, and extremely exhausted. I don't know how, but I somehow managed to call 911. A very cold, non-compassionate operator answered. She repeatedly kept insisting, "Are you sure he is dead?" I said, "Ma'am, I am a nurse. Yes, he is gone. Please get someone to my house." When the paramedics arrived shortly thereafter, they were very caring, the exact opposite of the 911 operator. They said they were not surprised by my experience. Apparently, they were familiar with this, and apologized for her attitude.

STILL IN SHOCK

Before the paramedics arrived, I called my daughter in Michigan, but then hung up on her and she had to call me right back. I do not remember hanging up until she told me later. I don't know how, but God! His grace was literally holding me up. It was as if I was on autopilot. I then called my daughter in Upstate New York and told her what nobody at any time ever wants to hear, that her dad was gone.

Cardiac arrest was put on the death certificate. The paramedics said, "Our experience has been that when this happens, the majority of the time when they find people on the floor, they are slumped over grabbing their chest."

Al wore a medic alert button around his neck which he could push at any time if he ever fell. A year prior, he had fallen without my knowledge and was on the floor for eighteen hours, barely alive, until I came home the next morning from a conference. Our doctor later said that he once had to amputate a person's limb after he was found lying on the floor for five hours due to a fall. Again, but God! So immediately, the medical alert button was ordered!

The paramedic asked, "Do you have any friends to call, because we don't want you to spend the night alone." I answered, "No, I don't have any friends," and was later gently rebuked by many wonderful friends. They also asked me if I had any clergy I wanted to call. Thank the Lord, I remembered our pastor's name. The paramedic called Pastor Phil Derstine and within less than an hour, he and his associate were at my front door. They stayed with me into the early morning hours, bringing much comfort, for which I am eternally grateful. He called one of the ladies from church to come and stay the night with me, not knowing that we already knew each other, for which I am also thankful.

Early the next day, a few friends who read about Al's passing on Facebook showed up at my doorstep. Their love and comfort will never be forgotten. They never called first, they just showed up. Do you know that is the very best thing you can do under these circumstances? Just simply show up! The one suffering most likely will not call, even if you are a well-meaning person and say, "Just call me if you need anything." My advice to anyone wondering about any type of so-called protocol would be this: forget about what you might think is proper or improper and "just do it!"

Love never fails. (1 Corinthians 13:8)

*My great grandchildren, Nora and Warren,
praying for me in June, 2017, shortly after
the death of their Papa*

A couple of hours later, my brother and sister-in-law drove two hours from South Florida. That timing was another divine appointment. They only spent part of their time in Florida, and I never knew when they were going to be here. They immediately rallied to the cause: running errands, picking my daughters up at the airport, and many other things.

Twenty-three hours later, both my daughters were at my doorstep. I greeted them at the door. We hugged and we cried. I then went to bed, because I had not slept for almost two days. It almost seemed surreal.

The rest of the family came from three different states, some staying a week or more. My house was filled with my amazing family. My little three-year-old great-granddaughter, Nora Elizabeth, said to her mother, "Why does everyone look sad?" When her mother explained it to her, she immediately went about the house giving comfort and showing compassion as only a child could, melting everyone's heart and bringing a smile to our faces.

"Let the children alone, and do not hinder them from coming to Me; for the kingdom of heaven belongs to such as these."

(Matthew 19:14)

I know that during this time, I was covered in a blanket of extravagant grace; which continued to flow so beautifully over my life. I did not realize then that up ahead, I would soon be encountering some very difficult and totally unexpected challenges.

Thank you, Lord, for grace; I like to call it extravagant grace!

His peace, which passes all understanding, enabled me to get up each day, get dressed, and function. There are "religious types" out there who might tend to be judgmental, thinking something along these lines: "You have the Lord, so you should be functioning very well and be happy that your loved one is in heaven and did not have to suffer. After all, you are a Christian." Thankfully, those kinds of comments were never made to me, but I know of others who have had that experience.

People have been very kind to me. My take on this is, if you don't know what to say, just be quiet. Someone once said, "Silence is golden." In certain scenarios, this could not be a more truthful statement. Oftentimes, you will find that just your loving presence is appreciated far more than you realize. You don't have to try to "fix it" because you can't anyway and spouting off a bunch of scriptures is not always the best approach. This is certainly not to put anyone under condemnation, because maybe some, if not all of us, have been guilty of doing one or more of these things. Those who have done these things are usually just trying to be helpful, not really knowing what to do. I have been guilty of these very things.

Everyone grieves/mourns differently.

"Blessed are those who mourn, for they shall be comforted."   (Matthew 5:4)

YOU CANNOT SPRINT THROUGH GRIEF

You are passing through this season of the valley of the shadow of death. You won't stay in this valley. The Lord gives everyone the time they need to grieve their losses and feel their pain as He heals their wounds and restores their soul. You are very significant to the King and His Kingdom, and you will come out stronger on the other side. He still has a powerful purpose for you.

I am here to tell you, and testify, that God has been the best husband to me in the whole wide world. There is none like Him! His love and amazing care for me, since my husband went to heaven, has been nothing short of astounding.

And the reproach of your widowhood you will remember no more. For your husband is your Maker, whose name is the Lord of hosts.
(Isaiah 54:4-5)

I am fully convinced that widows are very high on God's priority list!

Pure and undefiled religion in the sight of our God and Father is this: to visit orphans and widows in their distress, and to keep oneself unstained by the world. (James 1:27)

From the very moment my husband slipped into eternity, it seems the Lord went into overdrive on my behalf. He has been there for me in the smallest details of everyday life, like showing me how to fix things when I had no clue. He's often brought across my path just the "right person" at the "right time." He is continually revealing His lovingkindness by showing me His phenomenal care and extravagant love for the widow. All through this experience, He has so tenderly guided my steps; it's almost palpable.

But we do not want you to be uninformed,
brethren, about those who are asleep, so that
you will not grieve as do the rest who have
no hope. (1 Thessalonians 4:13)

As believers, we have hope!

How blessed is he whose help is the God of
Jacob, whose hope is in the Lord his God.
(Psalms 146:5)

You have undoubtedly heard of those without hope. They either have not heard or do not want to receive and accept the good news of the gospel. Andrew Wommack says, "It's the almost too good to be true news."[4]

"For God so loved the world, that He gave
His only begotten Son, that whoever believes
in Him shall not perish, but have eternal life."
(John 3:16)

Those with no hope have literally been seen throwing themselves on their loved ones' coffin while screaming and wailing.

The Scripture tells us that, "Whoever believes
in Him will not be disappointed."
(Romans 10:11)

My hope is in Christ and in His precious and magnificent promises. However, that does not mean I don't have moments of extreme sadness, which seem to come without warning and always in waves. In the beginning, after everyone was gone and I was all alone, I found myself walking in literal circles around my house. I don't even recall how long I would do this, maybe off and on for hours during the day. It seemed as if I was in a daze, just trying to process all that had taken place. You miss your loved ones beyond words; it's almost indescribable and at times unbearable…but God!

Six weeks after the death of my husband, my beloved, little dog, Precious, died. Oh no! This was almost too much to fathom. The vet said she saw this quite frequently in her practice after the death of an owner. Precious had just stopped eating, and rapidly went from nine pounds to six pounds, sitting all day long by my husband's chair. I tried to coach her with all her favorite foods. However, she would just look up at me with the saddest eyes. Wanting to please me, she would sniff the food and pretend to eat, but then would turn her head away.

Maybe you have felt the pain of a broken heart, a death, a divorce, a betrayal, or a child that has gone astray. Always try to remember,

> *The Lord is near to the brokenhearted, and*
> *saves those who are crushed in spirit.*
> (Psalms 34:18)

Yes, He is very close to you when you are broken and crushed.

I am still learning to navigate my way through this new season of life, and I will always and forever miss my husband of fifty-three years on this earth, but I have the blessed assurance that death is swallowed up in victory, and I will one day see him again.

> *Behold, I tell you a mystery; we will not all sleep, but we will all be changed, in a moment, in the twinkling of an eye, at the last trumpet; for the trumpet will sound, and the dead will be raised imperishable, and we will be changed. For this perishable must put on the imperishable, and this mortal must put on immortality; then will come about the saying that is written, "Death is swallowed up in victory. O death, where is your victory? O death, where is your sting?"*
> (1 Corinthians 15:51-55)

Death is an enemy.

The last enemy that will be abolished is
death. (1 Corinthians 15:26)

The Holy Spirit is our Comforter who never leaves us, fails us, or forsakes us. He knows the pain and sadness in our hearts when a loved one dies. Jesus felt the pain of Mary and Martha when their brother, Lazarus, died. All the while, He knew He would raise him from the dead after four days, yet "Jesus wept." (John 11:35) Though this is the shortest verse in the Bible, it is so profound. I am looking forward to that Great Day, that Glorious Day, where we will all be reunited once again, where there will be no more mourning, crying, or pain.

What a day that will be!

Oh, Happy Day, indeed!

"I am the resurrection and the life; he who
believes in Me will live even if he dies, and
everyone who lives and believes in Me will
never die." (John 11:25)

Al, looking toward heaven, taking in all the beauty
at Lake George, New York

Chapter 16

It's Never Too Late

The Lord will redeem everything that the enemy has stolen from you. I almost never stop smiling! That must make the devil really mad!

God gives you double for your trouble. He gives you beauty for ashes. He gives you the oil of joy instead of mourning. He gives you the mantle of praise instead of the spirit of heaviness. He comforts all those who mourn and sets the captives free. He gives you joy unspeakable and full of glory.

He fills you with His glorious Spirit so that you want to shout from the housetops: singing, and dancing, and praising His wonderful name! It has been said, *"It's never too late to have a happy childhood."*

> **The Lord will redeem everything that the enemy has stolen from you.**

Jumping for joy at the Great Wall of China

The very gifts and callings that God has put into you as a child will be the very thing the enemy will try to quench and squelch in your life. He and his demons come to do one thing only, and that is to steal, kill, and destroy all the good things that God has ordained for your life even before you were born.

> *Jesus said, "I came that they may have life,*
> *and have it abundantly."* (John 10:10)

> *"Since you are precious in My sight, since*
> *you are honored and I love you…."*
> (Isaiah 43:4)

OH, HAPPY DAY!

PRAYER OF SALVATION

If you do not know for sure if you will be going to heaven when you die, and you would like to know for sure, you can know today, right now, by simply praying this little prayer:

"Jesus, I repent of my sins, and ask you to come into my heart. I confess You as Lord and believe in my heart that God raised You from the dead."

Then I suggest that you quote the following Scripture passage:

If you confess with your mouth Jesus as Lord, and believe in your heart that God raised him from the dead, You will be saved; for with the heart a person believes, resulting in righteousness, and with the mouth he confesses, resulting in salvation. For the Scripture says, "Whoever believes in him will not be disappointed." (Romans 10:9-11)

If you prayed that simple prayer and quoted that Bible-promise, and you meant it from your heart, then your name will be included in the Lamb's Book of Life forever, and all of heaven is rejoicing!

Oh, Happy Day!!!

Christmas 2015
Al's last Christmas on earth with our Kentucky and Michigan family.

Christmas 2016
*Al's last Christmas in Florida, with our New York family;
just before he changed his address and moved to heaven.*

ABOUT THE AUTHOR

Sallie Yusko is an ordained minister and a retired registered nurse. She was married to the late Al Yusko for fifty-three years, and has two married daughters, six grandchildren, and two great-grandchildren.

She co-pastored with her husband in Upstate New York for fifteen years and then for six years in Bradenton, Florida. Al Yusko was a church planter, and through them both, numerous ministries were raised up and established under their covering, *More Than Conquerors Ministries International*.

Sallie has been gifted to minister to people in all walks of life, and she is able to cross all gender and denominational lines.

There is a powerful anointing that rests upon her, as she brings forth the Word and shares the bread of life. She has ministered on radio, television, prophetic conferences, retreats, and AGLOW International. Out of her experience was birthed a dynamic course, *Fashioning Women of Worth*. This course was a support group in the Upstate New York area that brought deliverance and healing to women and brought restoration to their souls.

You will be blessed, encouraged, challenged, and exhorted as she shares her life experiences with transparency, frankness, and humor, ministering Christ's love to all.

ENDNOTES

[1] www.poemofquotes.com/emilydickinson/pain-has-an-element-of-blank.php (accessed 5/14/2019).

[2] This statement was heard by the author during a message Bishop Chironna preached.

[3] http://www.essentialcslewis.com/confirming-c-s-lewis-quotations-series-overview/ (accessed 6/25/2019).

[4] The author heard Andrew Wommack say this frequently during his daily TV programs.

CONTACT INFORMATION

If you would like Sallie to speak or teach at any of your conferences, seminars, retreats, or workshops, she can be contacted by email: salliemary@gmail.com

Made in the USA
Middletown, DE
01 November 2019